Royal Pray

Royal Prayer

A Surprising History

DAVID BALDWIN

continuum

Published by the Continuum International Publishing Group

The Tower Building
11 York Road
London
SE1 7NX

80 Maiden Lane
Suite 704
New York
NY 10038

www.continuumbooks.com

First published 2009

British Library Cataloguing-in-Publication Data
A catalogue record for this book is available from the British Library.

ISBN 9780826423030

Designed and typeset by BookEns, Royston, Herts.
Printed and bound by MPG Books Ltd, Bodmin, Cornwall.

Contents

Introduction:
Royal Prayer – A Justification

In AD 57/8 St Paul wrote:

> Let every soul be subject unto the higher powers; for there is no power but of God: the powers that be are ordained of God. Whosoever therefore resisteth the power resisteth the ordinance of God: and they that resist shall receive unto themselves damnation. For rulers are not a terror to good works, but to the evil.[1]

In representing his or her people, a Monarch is at the same time both responsible and accountable to the People. This places the monarch with one foot at the edge of the realm of the known in company with the people – but the other in the realm of the mysterious unknown whose forces have been deemed by subjects to act upon their everyday lives. Thus the ancient Coronation Rite of the Sovereign includes the provision for Anointing of the Sovereign by the Archbishop of Canterbury:

> *in the form of a cross: On the palms of the hands, saying,* Be thy Hands anointed with holy Oil. *On the Breast, saying,* Be thy Breast anointed with holy Oil. *On the crown of the head, saying,* Be thy Head anointed with holy Oil: as Kings, priests, and prophets were anointed: And as Solomon was anointed king by Zadok the priest and Nathan the prophet, so be thou anointed, blessed, and consecrated Queen over the Peoples, whom the Lord thy God hath given thee to rule and govern, In the name of the Father, and of the Son, and of the Holy Ghost. Amen ... O Lord Jesus Christ, the Son of God, who by his Father was anointed with the Oil of gladness above his fellows, by his holy Anointing pour down upon your Head and Heart the blessing of

the Holy Ghost, and prosper the works of your Hands: that by the assistance of his heavenly grace you may govern and preserve the people committed to your charge in wealth, peace and godliness . . .[2]

The upshot is that monarchs have become appeasers of the unknown as advocates of their peoples. The monarch's role in invoking blessing upon particularly important events or things naturally results from this need. This is a direct and natural consequence of their duty of responsibility. On occasion the progression finds itself forced, as at the sixteenth-century Reformation when King Henry VIII assumed the responsibility in England of replacing the Holy Father in Rome's universal authority over 'his' Church to interface with the unknown realm of God.

There is very rare but tangible evidence of Henry VIII's own mind on his sacred duty as king to bring the teachings of the Bible to his subjects – and this before his sanctioning of Miles Coverdale's 1535/36 Bible in English and then the *Great Bible* of 1538 in English of which 9,000 copies had been produced by 1541 – but at an earlier point of no return in his determination to bring about his break with Rome over the governance of the Church in England. Only four complete, and three imperfect, books remain extant of Thomas Berthelet's Latin *Biblia Sacra* published in July 1535. Arthur Cayley pointed out in 1808 when producing his *Memoirs of Sir Thomas Moore* that Henry VIII was himself the personal author of the Preface to 'King's Printer' Berthelet's Bible. In this King Henry writes:

> We therefore, considering it our duty to God, have undertaken this task, as we should be within our realm like unto the soul in the body, and the sun in the universe, and exercise God's judgement as God's representative in our kingdom. And having everything in our power as regards jurisdiction, to seek always, in God's stead, to govern and protect the very Church itself; for whether her discipline grows or slackens, we are to render our account to Him, who entrusted her to us . . .'[3]

Such awesome responsibility, therefore, also brings with it the necessity to face and ride misfortunes born by Monarch and

Subject as they arise – flagged up necessarily as the failure of one or the other to accord with the will of the greater unknown. This is the realm of accountability of the Monarch to the subject. Those who invest the Monarch with a sacred quality in recognizing the God-given duty to represent them in the realms of the unknown have been more apt to retain monarchy despite the onset of disaster – though the regicide of King Charles I in 1648 constitutes a notable exception.

When things go wrong in a sacred system embracing all of society in which everyone has duties and responsibilities, someone has to take the blame for incurring the wrath of the Almighty – the King or his subjects. King Charles I lost his life as a consequence of Civil War, blamed by Oliver Cromwell and others for the consequences of his 'personal rule' and particular religious convictions. In finally severing his neck, Cromwell uttered the words 'dreadful necessity'.[4] But if Cromwell and Parliament, representing the people, were to blame the king for what had happened in the Realm, the people themselves did not get off Scot-free and were in turn rendered accountable for their regicidal action and subject to the possibility of divine retribution at the Restoration of the Monarchy in 1660. The Book of Common Prayer in 1662 included:

> A form of prayer with fasting to be used yearly on the Thirtieth of January, being the day of Martyrdom of the Blessed King Charles the First; to implore the mercy of God, that neither the guilt of that sacred and innocent blood, nor those other sins, by which God was provoked to deliver up both us and our King into the hands of cruel and unreasonable men, may at any time hereafter be visited upon us or our posterity.

The rubric allowed for a selection of sentences to be read, including that from Psalm ii, 2: 'The people stood up, and rulers took counsel together: against the Lord, and against his Anointed.' Blame was spread fairly wide in the subsequent prayer: 'We thy sinful creatures here assembled before thee, do, in the behalf of all the people of this land, humbly confess, that they were the crying sins of this Nation, which brought down this heavy judgement upon us.' The prayer also attempts to head off God's judgement upon the people for the bloodshed of regicide and civil war: 'lay it not to the charge of the people of this land; nor let it ever required of us or our posterity. Be merciful, O Lord, be merciful unto thy people, whom thou hast redeemed; and be not angry with us for ever'.

Elsewhere, monarchical systems of governance have gone to the wind in the face of secular principles of republican philosophy brought about by revolution. The United States of America in 1776, Russia in 1917 and France in 1789 and 1848 are examples over recent centuries.

Yet, even within such 'secular' systems of political governance, there is no getting away from responsibility. This is such an important concept that even heredity as an indication of the natural order of governance is tempered with the necessity for general consent as part of the Coronation ritual in Great Britain. The *Liber Regalis*, codified by Nicholas Lytlington,[5] Abbot of Westminster Abbey from 1362 to 1388, and used thereafter for Coronations, including rites from King Edgar's Coronation in 973 (used also for William the Conqueror in 1066), includes provision for 'Recognition' in which the

> Bishop that is to consecrate the king, shall address the people at the four sides of the stage, inquiring their will and consent about the consecration of the said king. The King meanwhile stands at his seat and turns himself to the four sides of the stage, as the Bishop addresses the people, who give their consent, as is customary, and with loud and unanimous shouts exclaim, *So be it, So be it,* and *Long live the king,* uttering with great joy the name of the King.

Without that, the monarch's role becomes somehow irregular or vulnerable to accusation of illegitimacy in representing the people.

But even just elected Heads of State or Members of a Parliament cannot hide from that same duty of representing their people. Just like a Monarch they can 'foul up' though, unlike monarchs, they can more easily leave the field of ultimate responsibility by relying upon the political system to remove them from office without a mammoth hiatus. This happens on a regular basis in the course of an election, or because they can resign or retire.

We shall see that royal prayers are no frivolous, fringe or irrelevant occurrences but rather have a place at the heart of many mainstream activities – and, moreover, have their exact parallel in systems of governance elsewhere that oddly proclaim themselves to be mercifully free of such trappings of monarchy.

Royal prayers, perhaps surprisingly to those who have not looked beyond the formalized constraints of the Prayer Book for them, in fact appear in welcome and regular use right across the mainstream of daily activity. The range is impressive despite detractors who misunderstand the reason for their inclusion and construct an inexact science to question their 'efficacy'.

What is not in doubt is the bravery of the Sovereign, along with the teaching around the Good Samaritan, in leading the way across stubborn social taboos that have left swathes of society disadvantaged. This was evident early on in Queen Elizabeth II's reign when she chose to visit a leper colony on the Oji River Settlement in Eastern Nigeria on 9 February 1956. In so doing she followed in the fearless footsteps of King Henry VI who in 1439 had stayed from 18 to 21 March as a resident of the Leper Hospital of St James's, on the site of the present St James's Palace in London. A year after this experience Henry VI publicly declared his intention of founding two colleges to provide good Christian education for the rising generation who would need to raise the wealth of the country in order, among other things, to tackle the circumstances of the disadvantaged. This understanding behind the founding of Eton College is perhaps less generally appreciated but was symbolized by King Henry VI granting perpetual custody of the Leper Hospital of St James's to the Provost of Eton College from 1450, upon the completion of the college – an arrangement that stood in place until leprosy became less common and King Henry VIII turned the site into a Palace from October 1531 when the Provost of Eton College turned over the buildings to him.

Even twentieth-century post-war reformers of the Coronation rituals in Norway saw the necessity, when abandoning coronation ritual, to retain a form of 'Benediction' upon a Sovereign

The Queen at the Oji River Settlement for lepers in Eastern Nigeria, 9 February 1956.
Photograph by David Moore, Camera Press, London.

faced with responsibility for an entire nation – recognizing that even the king himself is subject to a yet higher authority beyond the realm of mortal life.

The coronation paragraph in the Norwegian Constitution was dropped in 1908, thereby rendering the 1906 Coronation the last of its kind stretching back to Magnus V Erlingsson Bergen's at Christ Church in 1164. The last coronation involving anointing in Denmark took place in 1840, and that in Sweden in 1873 with King Oscar II and Queen Sophie. Although the Norwegian Parliament saw that the personal union with Sweden under which they were ruled under a joint king and diplomatic service had now dissolved as envisaged by constitutional reforms instituted in 1814, they failed to vote any process to replace that. And so Olav V himself took action upon the eve of his succession in 1958, advocating what he said five years earlier as Crown Prince:

> When you get married and found a family, it is a serious matter, and you are happy to kneel at the Lord's altar and be blessed with the laying on of hands and prayer. When you become a King, it is also a serious matter, and I would be happy

to kneel at the Lord's altar and be blessed with the laying on of hands and prayer.[6]

He further stated that he would like that to happen in the national sanctuary, by which he meant Trondheim Cathedral. This duly happened.

Of note was the specific request that those in charge of all three branches of government should be present, together with the chief of the armed forces. For this Benediction the Norwegian Crown was placed on the Altar of the Cross and the Royal Standard of 1906 and the ensign flown from HMS *Norfolk* (whose battle honours included *Bismark* and *Scharnhorst*) and which carried King Haakon VII back to Norway from Britain in 1945, were placed on the steps to the High Altar.

Much the same process was repeated at the Benediction of King Harald V and Queen Sonja on 23 June 1991. The wording of the Benediction this time around was to:

Bless King Harald V, strengthen him and guide him in his work as Norway's King. Let our King with his people live in freedom and peace under your gracious hand. We ask you: may King Harald pursue his high vocation with wisdom and justice, and maintain truth and law in keeping with your will and with the people's laws. Sustain him by your mercy if evil days should come, and be yourself his strength and joy. We ask this in Jesus's name.

In the Benediction of the Queen there was also an appeal: 'God of all joy, look with favour on Queen Sonja. May her work support the King's work. Help her to use her talents and strength to the joy and benefit of Norway's land and people.'

The conclusion is that monarchy continues to fulfil a vital, pivotal, role in protecting the interests of a people or nation.

Notes

[1] Rom. 13, 1–2..
[2] 'The Form and Order of Her Majesty's Coronation' in E. Ratcliffe, *The Coronation Service of Her Majesty Queen Elizabeth II* (London: SPCK, 1953) – 'will help all listeners and viewers to follow the broadcast ceremonies'.

[3] Henry was evidently influenced by Erasmus's *Institutio Principis Christiani* of 1516. Erasmus wrote: 'Quod Deus in universo, quod sol in mundo, quod oculus in corpore, hoc oportet esse Principem in Republica', whereas Henry substitutes 'anima' (i.e. soul) for 'oculus' (i.e. eyes) of the body when writing 'ut in regno simus sicut Anima in corpore et Sol in mundo'. Henry thereby adduces to himself the deeper responsibility under God of custodian of the very soul of the Church.

That so few examples of the Berthelet's 1535 Bible survive may indicate it was abandoned at publication – perhaps not surprisingly as Henry provoked shock in setting about the beheading of John Fisher at Tower Hill on 22 June, followed closely by Thomas Moore on 6 July. Cromwell's instruction of 1538 stated that the *Great Bible* be displayed in every parish church, containing as it did a highly illustrated preface requiring the reader to track back the pictorial origin of the repeated motif 'Verbum Dei' from the parishioners through the great officers of the Church (the Archbishop of Canterbury and Thomas Cromwell), to King Henry himself and ultimately to God. The British Library possesses a copy, BL C.18.d.10, which was probably King Henry VIII's own personal copy.

[4] Dr George Bates, Physician to Charles I, stated of the King's body lying at St James's Palace from the following day: 'Cromwell, that he might to the full glut his traitorous eyes with that spectacle, having opened the coffin wherein the King's body was carried from the scaffold into the Palace, curiously viewed it, and with his finger severed the head from the shoulder, as we have been informed by eye-witnesses.' A more contrite reaction is that recording Cromwell as uttering 'dreadful necessity' upon that occasion.

[5] MS '*Liber Regalis ...*', Abbot Lytlington, *c.*1390, Muniment Room, Westminster Abbey. Transcribed as '*Liber Regalis seu ordo consecrandi regem solum. Ordo consecrandi reginam cum rege. Ordo consecrandi reginam solam. Rubrica de Regis exequiis.E. codice Westmonasteriensi editus*', Roxburghe Club, 1870.

[6] Conversation between Crown Prince Olav and Bishop Arne Fjellbu on St.Olav's Feast at Trondheim in 1953 quoted in G.T. Risasen, *The Norwegian Crown Regalia* (Nidaros Domkirkes Restaureringsarbeider, 2006), p. 50.

1

Royal Launching and Christening of Ships

There has been an intimate association of royalty with boats down the aeons. Moses was placed in a basket of papyrus reeds and launched in the Nile – the Hebrew word for basket being used in the Bible only twice: in this instance with a river, and in describing the cypress wood ark of Noah, both being covered with bitumen imported from the Dead Sea – and in the case of Moses' 'basket' launched into the Nile to be found by Pharaoh's daughter, the future eighteenth dynasty princess who was to become Queen Hatchepsut. But around 2,350 years earlier there was the example of Sargon, King of Akkad, who wrote in *c.*3800: 'my lowly mother conceived me, in secret she brought me forth. She set me in a basket of rushes, with bitumen she closed my door. She cast me into the River, which rose not over me ... Akki, the irrigator, as his own son reared me'.

The elaborate Palaces of the Minoan civilization on Crete were synonymous with shipping and trading outposts to support the enormous expense of their building and upkeep, but, more particularly, warships were chosen to defend the surrounding waters rather than building defensive walls around the palace complexes (so elaborate that the Minotaur in its maze at Knossos became symbolic of the sheer size of the palaces).

The association of royalty with the sea often resulted in the ship and crew becoming an extension of the sovereign himself. Thus King Joao II of Portugal equipped the explorer Diogo Cao with limestone pillars quarried from Alcantara, capped with a cross on a cube of stone that bore the Royal Arms, to mark out claims to territory. Part of that which Cao set up at Santa Maria (on the present day Angolan coast) in 1482 was retrieved and taken back to Lisbon, where its inscription may be read:

In the year 6681, from the creation of the world, and 1482 from the birth of Our Lord, Jesus Christ, the most high, most excellent prince King Joao, the second of Portugal, ordered this land to be discovered and these pillars to be set up by Diogo Cao, squire of his household.

Just five years later King Joao II issued orders to two Arabic-speaking explorers, Pedro de Civilha in his Royal Household, and Alfonso de Pavia, to search for a sea route to India, issuing them with a Carta de Marear copied from a chart of the world drawn in 1428 (itself according to Gavin Menzies taken from the Pizzigano Chart of 1424 and therefore of Chinese origin).

King Joao knew therefore that the Cape of Good Hope had already been 'discovered', though Bartholomew Dias is credited with doing so in 1487. As it happens, the Chinese had been trading westward across the Indian Ocean to the east coast of Africa since the Tang Dynasty (AD 618–907) and traded in porcelain as far south as Sofala, with chronicles left by Ma Huan and Fei Xin who sailed on five voyages before 1421. The clinching evidence of trade with East Africa in practical navigational terms is the extant rutter of Wui Pei Chi with its sailing directions for reaching East Africa from China. But voyagers from China, unless they were Nestorians,[1] were not interpreting their endeavours in the context of Christianity, and had no 'baggage' of archaic prohibitions with which to reconcile what they saw, did, and expected to see.

With regard to Christendom, mariners have in general challenged the Church more than the Monarch when it comes to the 'truths' they represent as they have crossed horizons of discovery and seen for the first time with their own eyes things hitherto denied by the Church. Ferdinand Magellan set off in 1519 from Spain on his circumnavigatory voyage with the statement that: 'The Church says that the earth is flat, but I know that it is round, for I have seen the shadow on the moon, and I have more faith in a shadow than in the Church.'

Yet the actions of the elements and curious coincidences down the ages far outstripping mathematical probability have effectively removed such confidence mariners might have otherwise had in their own ability to the extent that they understood that happenstance often looked to be the work of something sacred – spiritual realms beyond the geographically or meteorologically discoverable or explicable, whose blessing on their activities or intentions needed to be invoked, and fatal wrath deflected. Here enters the Monarch and the Church in their natural roles of responsibility as advocates or intercessors for their peoples between God and man.

As it turns out, Christopher Marlow's question in *Doctor Faustus* relating to the classical 'Helen of Greece ... Was this the face that launched a thousand ships and burnt the topless towers of Ilium?' turns out to be truer of the modern monarchy's contribution to maritime activity. Egyptians, Greeks and Romans all appealed to their gods to protect seamen. Poseidon in Greek mythology (Neptune in Roman) was the object of these supplications. Ship-launching in classical Greece involved participants wreathing their heads with olive branches, drinking wine to honour the gods and the pouring of water on the new vessel as a symbol of blessing. Shrines were carried on board Greek and Roman ships; a practice extended into the Middle Ages. The shrine was usually placed upon the quarterdeck, which for that reason continues to have sacred significance to sailors.

The earliest forms of medieval Christian ritual applied in the world of shipping to invoke blessing took the form of a priest sprinkling holy water on the deck of a vessel in the direction of the four corners of the compass, together with invocatory prayers for the well-being of the vessel and its crew, and the shrine placed on the quarterdeck. The Ottoman Empire practice also involved an appeal to the divine, with the sacrificing of a sheep on the deck in accordance with Muslim ritual, followed by fasting.

The justification for the Christian practice lay in Jesus's ability to calm the raging waves upon the Sea of Galilee that so terrified his disciples while he slept. The rubric for the Royal Naval Act of Dedication of a vessel includes this Gospel account from St Mark, 4.36-41, concluding:

And he was in the hinder part of the ship, sleeping upon a pillow. And they awake him and say to him: Master, doth it not concern thee that we perish? And rising up, he rebuked the wind and said to the sea: Peace. Be still, And the wind ceased; and there was a great calm. And he said to them: Why are you fearful? Have you not faith yet? And they feared exceedingly. And they said to one another: Who is this (thinkest thou) that both the wind and sea obey him?

Likewise the Acts of the Apostles constitutes the justification for the Church's role in maritime affairs in recording Paul's imminent shipwreck off Malta, when he stood up on the rolling deck to caution the centurion Julius and his terrified crew with the words:

> Men, you should have taken my advice not to sail from Crete; then you would have spared yourselves this damage and loss. But now I urge you to keep up your courage, because not one of you will be lost; only the ship will be destroyed. Last night an angel of the God whose I am and whom I serve stood beside me … have faith that it will happen just as he told me. Nevertheless, we must run aground on some island.

The vessel broke up in the waves smashing the Maltese coast but St Paul and the entire crew survived as he prophesied.

Maritime peoples have tended to call upon their representatives, hereditary or elected, with much the same request: for safety at sea and for the sea to protect them.

The Venetians, whose form of governance in mediaeval days veered between the Doge being effectively elected by a common franchise or from time to time instead by a restricted elite of hereditary patriciate, went further than most, perhaps because they owed their very existence to the sea to whose lagoons they fled from AD 375 to protect themselves from the marauding Huns and Visigoths. A direct consequence of this and the total dependence of the Venetians upon the sea surrounding their lagoon for their livelihood, trade and subsequent empire, was the ceremony known as the 'Sposalizio del Mare' – Marriage with the Sea.

At the close of the tenth century, to commemorate Ventian control of Dalmatia, Doge Pietro Orseolo (AD 991–1008) created a ceremony involving a combination of the Doge, City authorities, clergy and people going to the port of San Nicolo di Lido on Ascension Day for a blessing of the Adriatic Sea.

For this the Doge was dressed in gold and ermine robes, with corno atop, and sailed in the most elaborately carved and gilded galley called the Bucintoro ('bucin' being a many oared boat and 'di oro' meaning gilded with gold) to the harbour mouth of San Nicolo on the Lido, where he was joined by the Patriarch. Here the Doge threw the 'wedding' ring, first donated by Alexander III in 1177 in gratitude for Venice's role in reconciling the papacy with the Imperial empire, onto the waters, at the same time pronouncing the prayer: 'We marry you, O sea, in a sign of true and perpetual dominion, asking God to protect those who travel by sea.' Alexander had given the ring in recognition of the Venetian Republic's dominion over the sea, likening the relationship as a bride to a groom. Taking this literally, the Senate decreed the construction of a Bicintoro 'quod fabricentur navilium ducentorum hominum' for the annual commemoration, the first of which was launched in 1277 and the last, under Doge Alvise Mocenigo, on 12 January 1728. Paralleling the British Sovereign personifying Justice by means of the sacred conferral of the Sword of Justice at the Coronation, the Doge's Bucintoro in the sixteenth century had a statue mounted on the prow called the 'Venezia in Giustizia' (i.e. 'Venice in Justice')

Later it was sometimes the practice for the Patriarch to bless the ring but for the Doge to pour a bucket of holy water into the sea instead of the ring. A number of these rings survive, together with remnants of the last Bucintoro which was desecrated by the French invaders in 1797, the hull being used as a prison ship to humiliate the Venetians. A magnificent model of the Bucintoro is to be seen at the Museo Storico Navale, where also are to be found similar rings surviving from the launching of modern Italian warships.[2] From 1866 every ship launched in the Arsenal shipyard had a bronze ring secured by ribbon to the stern so that the ring touched the water as the ship descended down the slipway thus renewing the marriage with the sea. These rings were recovered and preserved in decorated coffers, a large collection of which are displayed in the Museo Storico Navale.

A modern version of the ceremony is still kept on the First

Sunday after Feast of the Ascension persists, these days with the Mayor sailing to the traditional spot in the San Nicolo in decorated boat to throw a laurel wreath into the lagoon.

The Church representing such a potent force in the face of nature, ship christening has survived as an integral element of launching and commissioning, though the onset of the English Reformation did see an initial diminution of the clergy's role in favour of the royal family, which imbalance was to last for two and a half centuries or so, and in some other European Protestant countries, before Anglican Church and Monarchy 'teamed up' again for such occasions.

Thus the christening party for the launch of the 64-gun ship-of-the-line *Prince Royal* in 1610 included the Prince of Wales and naval architect Phineas Pett, who was master shipwright at the Woolwich yard. Pett described the proceedings thus:

> The noble Prince ... accompanied with the Lord Admiral and the great lords, were on the poop, where the standing great gilt cup was ready filled with wine to name the ship so soon as she had been afloat, according to ancient custom and ceremony performed at such times, and heaving the standing cup overboard. His Highness then standing upon the poop with a selected company only, besides the trumpeters, with a great deal of expression of princely joy, and with the ceremony of drinking in the standing cup, threw all the wine forwards towards the half-deck, and solemnly calling her by name of the Prince Royal, the trumpets sounding the while, with many gracious words to me, gave the standing cup into my hands.

The 'standing cup' was a large cup fashioned of precious metal. When the ship began to slide down the ways, the presiding officer took a ceremonial sip of wine from the cup, and poured the rest on the deck or over the bow. Until Charles II's day the cup was thrown overboard and belonged to the retriever, but thereafter it was presented to the master shipwright. The National Maritime Museum has in its collection a tankard inscribed: 'At the launching of His Majestes Ship the Captain a 3rd rate of 70 Guns 1230 Tuns ye 14 of April 1743. Built by Mr John Holland at Woolwich.'

Meanwhile abroad, where the liturgical aspects of ship

christenings continued unabated in Roman Catholic countries, Royal Navy Chaplain, the Revd Henry Teonge, left a record in 1675 of the launch by the Knights of Malta of a 'briganteen of 23 oars':

> Two fryers and an attendant went into the vessel, and kneeling down prayed halfe an houre, and layd their hands on every mast, and other places of the vessel, and sprinkled her all over with holy water. Then they came out and hoysted a pendent to signify she was a man of war; then at once thrust her into the water.

In Hanoverian Britain the 'standing cup' ceremony was replaced by the practice of breaking a bottle across the bow, the first recorded case being one of the Princesses of Hanover who threw the bottle herself, though missing the ship entirely and injuring one of the spectators at the launch (who subsequently put in a claim for damages against the Admiralty). Significantly, from 1810 a lady was usually asked to perform the ceremony.

Although 'sponsors' of English warships were customarily members of the royal family, senior naval officers or Admiralty officials, a few civilians were invited to sponsor Royal Navy ships during the nineteenth century.

Finally, in 1875, the religious element returned to naval christenings with Princess Alexandra, wife of the Prince of Wales, personally introducing an Anglican choral service at the launching ceremony for the battleship HMS *Alexandra*. The usage continues to this day with the singing of Psalm 107, incorporating its special meaning to mariners:

> They that go down to the sea in ships;
> And occupy their business in great waters;
> These men see the works of the Lord,
> and His wonders in the deep

It had been intended to call the ship HMS *Superb*, but the name was changed to *Alexandra* at her launching. It was an immensely important event to naval architecture for *Alexandra* was the first British ironclad to be launched by a member of the royal family; the Duke and Duchess of Edinburgh, the Duke and Duchess of Teck and the Duke of Cambridge were also present.

HRH Princess Alexandra naming HMS Alexandra, 1875. Image unattributed

HMS Alexandra, c.1880s

The involvement and royal prayers of the modern British monarchy are to be found across a spectacularly wide range of the daily life and work of maritime Britain – not just in the occasional launch of a huge great trans-oceanic liner. Royal prayers are to be found in the endeavours of the life-saving Royal National Lifeboat Institution (RNLI); the marking of hazards to shipping and the provision of navigational aids around the entire coastline through the activities of Trinity House and the Northern Lights; the opening of docks, bridges and coastguard facilities; and of course royal prayers have been invoked at the launching of particular ships that have been designed to revolutionize naval maritime operations or trade.

The Queen and her forbears have maintained a special relationship with the Royal Navy. Every warship is styled Her Majesty's Ship (HMS) and the monarch's prayers have been offered at the launch of some which have turned out to inhabit the most unusual ship's lives, often with global results.

Warships bearing the name *Dreadnought* are a case in point. That launched by King Edward VII on 10 February 1906 was the first of the famous new generation of Battleship built partly as response to the German navy's expansion since 1898. The British government's adoption of the policy of 'two power standing' required that the British fleet should outnumber the combined fleets of two other powers. As Germany built more ships, so Britain responded in accordance with this principle. The launching was described thus by the *Guardian* correspondent in the issue of 12 February 1906, the King wearing the uniform of Admiral of the Fleet:

> Sir John Fisher, wearing the crimson ribbon of the Bath, attended the King closely throughout the ceremony. The dockyard chaplain conducted the religious service observed at the birth of our ships of war. The singing of the choir was lost in the wind, but the voice of the Bishop of Winchester pronouncing a benediction was distinctly heard in a lull. Afterwards came the profaner music from the workmen. An unusually loud chorus from the standing ways attracted the King's curiosity, and with Lord Tweedmouth and Sir John Fisher he moved out to the end of the platform and gazed

down on the crowd of little white figures that swarmed beneath the great curve of the ship.

Immediately the King was seen there was a loud roar of welcome, the workmen hammering their tools on whatever was to hand. At this moment Admiral Barry came with word that all was ready. The King turned and walked into the little stall and grasped the flower-decked bottle of wine that was held in its place by a cord above and another to the bows below, attached to a running weight in the shape of a golden crown. The King pulled out the bottle and let it go, but the flowers prevented it from breaking. A second attempt cracked it, and the wine trickled down the grey bows.

The launch and commissioning of this ship revolutionized naval technology worldwide.

Fifty-four years later, in 1960, Her Majesty The Queen launched the next HMS *Dreadnought* – this time Britain's first nuclear-powered submarine. The construction of *Dreadnought* was occasioned by the launch in the Unitead Staes of America of the world's first nuclear-powered submarine, *Nautilus*, by Mamie Eisenhower in 1954 – so important was the design seen to be to the history of future marine propulsion. *Nautilus* sailed on her maiden voyage in 1955 broadcasting the immortal words 'underway on nuclear power' and a new era of propulsion had begun. It was personal friendship between *Nautilus*'s master-mind, Admiral Rickover and Lord Louis Mountbatten of Burma (First Sea Lord 1955–59) that resulted in the ability of Britain to match this by successfully incorporating an American Westinghouse nuclear reactor in *Dreadnought*'s bows. The keel of *Dreadnought* was laid at Vickers's Barrow-in-Furness yard on the 12 June 1959 by HRH The Duke of Edinburgh and she was launched by HM The Queen on Trafalgar Day (21 October) 1960 with exactly the same traditional prayer as her predecessor.

Dreadnought had a most eventful life, surfacing at the North Pole on 3 March 1971. Perhaps her most important peace-keeping mission is shrouded in mystery. In 1977 she attended the Silver Jubilee Fleet Review off Spithead but soon after, in November 1977, she sped to the Falkland Islands as part of a secret taskforce which included the frigates *Alacrity* and *Phoebe*

HMS Dreadnought. Royal Navy (Ministry of Defence)

and Royal Fleet Auxiliaries (RFAs) *Resource* and *Olwen*. The mission, codenamed 'Operation Journeyman', was devised to deter imminent Argentine aggression and prevent a feared invasion of the South Atlantic Islands, which were a Dependent Territory of the Crown.[3] *Dreadnought* was given orders by Prime Minister Jim Callaghan to surface deliberately near an Argentine vessel in the South Atlantic.[4] This turned out to be a merchant ship that flashed a frantic signal to Buenos Aires, thus deterring Argentina from invading the Falklands five years before Argentina's initially successful second attempt in 1982. Although *Dreadnought* had been decommissioned in some secrecy in 1980 her design drawings had been betrayed to the Soviet Union by the Portland spy ring in the 1960s.

British Royal Naval nuclear propulsion has, itself, undergone a technological revolution and so it was natural that a member of the royal family be summoned to offer the royal prayer at the christening of the first of the new class of nuclear-powered submarine incorporating this technology – HMS *Astute*. On this occasion the Christening of the nuclear-powered submarine was led by the Rt Revd Graham Dow, Bishop of Carlisle, and she was launched with the traditional prayer by HRH The Duchess of Cornwall, on 8 June 2007.

The Bishop of Carlisle recorded:

Launch of HMS Astute by HRH The Duchess of Cornwall, 2007. Ceremony included blessing by the Rt Revd Graham Dow, Bishop of Carlisle. Photograph: Church Times issue 7530, 6 July 2007

HMS Astute in trials, following launch by HRH The Duchess of Cornwall, 2007. Royal Navy (MOD) Photograph Gallery

I led a service for the blessing of the nuclear-propelled submarine HMS Astute last month in the BAE Systems shipyard at Barrow . . .

The Church accepts the need for military forces, and my involvement with the event signified a positive connection between God and the need for them. If it is held that the Church should refrain from any blessing of Her Majesty's forces, then it should withdraw its chaplains. Like any other naval ship, Astute is a tool for the good military purposes of defending the country, preserving freedom, and maintaining peace.

In the bases where the submarine will dock, the crew will be relating to the Royal Navy chaplaincy provision. It would be strange to support the ministry of naval chaplains, but then to say that the Bishop should not pray at the launch of the submarine . . . I prayed:

'This ship and those who serve in her may, in the course of her life, be in times of great danger. And since none of us can be faithful to the high trust placed in us without the help of God, let us join together in thanksgiving for those engaged in building her, and seek God's blessing on Astute and on all who serve in her in the years to come.

O Lord God Almighty, we thank you for all the skills and the sustained effort through which this ship has been built. Let your blessing be upon her and upon all who serve and sail in her. May your hand always protect them and direct their ways. May they work together in safety as one team, in harmony and mutual support. May this ship serve the good of all humanity and be a support to those who seek to live in peace, now and in the years ahead. Amen.'

It took a further year and a half to fit out the submarine, and to install her nuclear reactor core, before her return to the Buccleuch Dock, and at that point in November 2008 HRH The Duchess of Cornwall paid another visit to speak to the ship's company and her BAE engineers. Her intention was to familiarize herself with what living and sleeping next to a nuclear reactor for long deployments will mean for the sailors, especially when it comes to 'fighting the ship', and to meet the families of the serving crew who are supporting them. As godmother to the ship she will now be involved in her welfare and future operations

The royal family had in fact contributed prayers to the endeavours of the Royal Navy throughout the Cold War years of nuclear stand-off between the Great Powers following the end of the Second World War.

With the development of missile surface-to-air defence as a more effective substitute for gunnery, in 1960 HRH Princess Alexandra launched HMS *Devonshire*, the first operational County Class destroyer – the first true warship of the missile age – equipped with Sea Cat and Sea Slug guided missiles. For the next two decades, through the Cold War, this Class of eight constituted the Fleet's first line of defence against air attack. HMS *Devonshire* was re-commissioned again by HRH Princess Alexandra in 1975, and two of the Class subsequently saw intense action, one with total loss, in the 1982 Falklands War. *Devonshire* was eventually sunk as a target ship in the Atlantic by Sea Harriers in 1984, the eighth to bear the name.

Commissioning and re-commissioning of Her Majesty's Ships is a Christian ceremony, and is taken very seriously. An ecumenical rubric is employed. That used for the recommissioning of the destroyer HMS *Daring* in 1966 at Devonport opened with the Captain reading the Warrant and addressing the ship's company, in the presence of HRH Princess Alexandra, thus:

> Seeing that in the course of our duty we are set in the midst of many and great dangers and that we cannot be faithful to the high trust placed in us without the help of Almighty God, let us unite our prayers in seeking his blessing upon this ship and all who serve in her, that she may sail under God's good providence and protection, and that there may never be lacking men well-qualified to offer in her their work and skill for his greater glory, and for the protection of our realm and dominions.

> The Captain shall call on the Ship's Company to ask for God's Blessing on the ship, using this ancient call from the Gaelic Blessing 1589:

> *The Captain:* I call upon you to pray for God's blessing on this ship. May God the Father bless her.

Ship's Company: Bless our ship.
The Captain: May Jesus Christ bless her.
Ship's Company: Bless our ship.
The Captain: May the Holy Spirit bless her.
Ship's Company: Bless our ship.
The Captain: What do ye fear, seeing that God the Father is with you?
Ship's Company: We fear nothing.
The Captain: What do ye fear, seeing that God the Son is with you?
Ship's Company: We fear nothing.
The Captain: What do ye fear, seeing that God the Holy Spirit is with you?
Ship's Company: We fear nothing.

After hymns and other prayers the ceremony ended with the prayer 'God Save The Queen'.[5]

In an official interview with the Chaplain-General, the Venerable Stephen Robbins, in October 2008, for the journal *Defence Focus*, the question was posed: 'Britain's population is increasingly either non-religious or follows other faiths. If this continues, will it threaten the principle of a Christian Army, where recruits swear allegiance to God and to the Queen?' the Chaplain General replied:

> Recruits swear allegiance to the Queen through God. Will it threaten it? I don't know, only time can tell. I suppose Britain's Armed Forces could theoretically become secular as lots of other countries have done, but if we do, I think there will still be a place for Christianity but it might be different from today.

Christening of HM Yacht *Britannia* and Launch by The Queen

In 1953 at the launching of HM Yacht *Britannia*, there was a Christening service conducted by the Revd John Mackay and The Queen launched the vessel with her prayer: 'I name this ship Britannia and God bless all who sail in her', using a bottle of Empire wine instead of the traditional champagne for the naming, symbolizing that the Royal Yacht was to be the link with the Commonwealth. Until the launching ceremony for the Royal Yacht *Victoria and Albert* in 1899, it had been the practice to launch Royal Yachts in advance of blessing them at a later date.

But the Royal Yacht was also a non-combatant ship of the Royal Navy – a fact noted by Minic Models who produced a waterline model toy of her to go with others of the current fleet, which could be purchased in either her standard blue and white hull and superstructure with gold funnel, or else in white all over with a large red cross on the funnel in her capacity as a hospital ship.

She was deployed as just that in the Yemen crisis of 1986 when at 6.25 p.m. on 17 January *Britannia* ignored a challenge from nearby Soviet vessels *Boris Chilikin* (a Ropucha Class landing ship) and an Ugra Class vessel (submarine support ship) not to enter Yemeni territorial waters, and steamed into Khormaksar bay, broke out large Union flags at each mast, floodlit the superstructure and picked up a total of 152 people of 26 nationalities and one French dog. HMS *Newcastle*, HMS *Juniper* and RFA *Brambleleaf* of the Armilla Patrol, together with HMS *Hydra* of the Royal Naval Hydrographic Department surveying off East Africa, steamed to a rendezvous point over the horizon near a French destroyer, *Da Grasse*. Upon hearing of the rescue of the dog, the carpenter aboard HMS *Newcastle* fashioned a wooden lamp post which was transferred for use aboard *Britannia*. The operation resumed the next day but had to be suspended when the crew of *Britannia*'s 30-foot pinnace were subjected to sniper fire, but resumed for half an hour until tanks appeared on the beach. Flag Officer Royal Yacht, Admiral Garnier, recorded that: 'it was a little like watching the Royal Tournament because we could see the rebel tanks coming in from one side and firing over the top of the Yacht's boats while Government tanks were responding from the other side'.[6]

Yet *Britannia* had managed to rescue another 279 people, including the Ambassador.[7] This left 160 people on the beach as the rebel forces launched their final assault on Aden. Although *Britannia* returned to the coast having offloaded French nationals to their warships, shells were landing in the sea between her and the shore, so she steamed across to Djibuti to offload more of the rescued and returned by night to a different shoreline at Zinjibar whence it was learned that the remaining evacuees and others had fled under duress. *Britannia* picked up 209 from this location and then steamed into international waters to offload these to HMS *Jupiter*. Next morning *Britannia* steamed into Little Aden to pick up 15 starving British nationals, and then hosted a meeting between Soviet and French naval officers aboard to coordinate future action. This resulted in some success, with merchant vessels arriving, though still no Yemeni authority would permit warships to enter Yemeni waters. *Britannia* had to rescue a further 227 people on 22 January from Little Aden rather than Khormaksar because of the sea swell. On 23 January *Britannia* rescued her final 200 people and headed for Djibuti on the East African coast, only to learn within half an hour of steaming that another Briton had turned up at the beach to be rescued – one Yemen-born London bus driver, Saleh Ali. *Britannia* turned back and Ali recorded: 'when I saw the launch coming in, with its White Ensign fluttering in the wind, I was very happy inside and there were tears in my eyes. The Queen's yacht turned back for me, just for me'.[8]

Britannia was finally decommissioned in 1997 after 44 years of service and 1,087,623 miles of steaming, with no analysis of the enormous financial benefits to the UK taxpayer and the UK balance of payments through the encouragement of trade which she had earned by her status as royal host around the world. She now lies at Leith's Ocean Terminal.

The ship's communion set, comprising silver chalice of small bowl atop a conical stem, two conical cruet and a pyx, was 'Presented to Her Majesty Queen Elizabeth II by the Chamber of Shipping of the United Kingdom 1964' as stated on its special box, and is now deployed for use at the Domestic Chapel in Kensington Palace.

Lifeboats

Royal prayer associated with regular life-saving endeavours includes support of the voluntary-funded Royal National Lifeboat Institution. HM The Queen launched the RNLI *Richard Cox Scott* during a visit to Falmouth in 2002, her Golden Jubilee year, in the course of which The Queen and the Duke of Edinburgh also visited the Maritime Museum where a small yacht, *Bluebottle*, given to them by the Island Sailing Club of Cowes in 1948 as a wedding present, is now an exhibit. Following this, The Queen named what was at the time the RNLI's latest lifeboat, praying: 'I name this lifeboat Richard Cox Scott. May God bless her and all who sail in her.' On the quayside, a Royal Marines band played the theme from *Thunderbirds* as The Queen and the Duke of Edinburgh boarded the lifeboat for a harbour trip.

Trinity House and Northern Lights

Another sphere of royal prayer activity is to be found in today's workings of Trinity House and the Northern Lights – work essential to the daily maritime trade of the UK.

On the 17 October 2007 Her Majesty The Queen officially named Trinity House's new vessel, THV *Galatea*, praying 'I name this ship *Galatea*. May God bless her and all who sail in her' before releasing a bottle of 'Pol Roger Sir Winston Churchill Cuvée' champagne on the side of the vessel. The Duke of Edinburgh, the Master of Trinity House, presided over the ceremony, which was conducted aboard the vessel moored alongside HMS *Belfast* in the River Thames. The Master of Trinity then invited the Rt Revd and Rt Hon. Richard Chartres to bless the vessel, which is deployed in buoy handling, wreck marking, towing and multi-beam and side-scan hydrographic surveying.

In February 2007, the Duke of Edinburgh became the longest serving Master of Trinity House in its 500-year history. Sir Winston Churchill was an Elder Brother of Trinity House until his death in 1965 and Pol Roger was his favourite champagne. THV *Galatea* is the second ship of that name in the history of the Trinity House fleet; the first being a large paddle yacht built in 1868 which served Trinity House well until 1895, during which she aided in the commissioning of the life-saving Eddystone and Wolf Rock lighthouses, and attended the sovereign handover of Heligoland lighthouse in the North Frisian Islands to Germany

Trinity House Vessel Galatea named by The Queen in the presence of
HRH The Duke of Edinburgh and he Rt Revd and Rt Hon. Richard Chartres,
Lord Bishop of London

in 1894, consequent upon the 1890 Treaty ceding British sovereignty over Heligoland to Germany in exchange for Zanzibar.

Oceanic Liners

Royal prayer has found greater publicity in the launching of larger vessels of the mercantile marine, especially oceanic liners.

On Monday 10 December 2007 HRH The Duchess of Cornwall maintained the traditional royal prayer at her launching of Cunard's *Queen Victoria*: 'May God bless her, and all who sail in her'. Approximately 2000 attendees, including HRH The Prince of Wales and Carol Marlow, President of Cunard, watched. It took the assistance of a crewman aboard to ensure the bottle of champagne broke. Speaking of the recent expansion of the fleet which includes *Queen Mary 2*, and *Queen Elizabeth* which will be launched in 2010, the Cunard President Marlow said: 'Three new ships in six years ... this, ladies and gentlemen, is a revival. Cunard's lion does roar again.'

There had been an earlier attempt by Cunard in 1934 to name a liner *Queen Victoria*. Until her launch she was known simply as *Cunard Hull No. 534*, her intended name being kept a closely guarded secret. Felix Morley, in 1936 editor of the *Washington Post* and a guest of Cunard on the vessel's maiden voyage, recalled sitting next to Sir Percy Bates, Chairman of the Cunard Line, in the course of which Bates told him the story of the naming of the ship upon which they were sailing 'on condition you won't print it during my lifetime'. In his 1979 autobiography, *For the Record*, Morley wrote that Bates confided in him during that maiden voyage that Cunard intended to name the ship *Victoria*, in keeping with company tradition of giving its ships names ending in 'ia'. However, when company representatives asked the King's permission to name the ocean liner after Britain's 'greatest queen', he said his wife, Queen Mary, would be delighted. The Cunard delegation had of course no other choice but to report that *Cunard Hull No. 534* would be called RMS *Queen Mary*.

But there was already a Clyde turbine steamer named *Queen Mary* (now preserved alongside the Embankment of the River Thames), so Cunard White Star had to reach a compromise with the owners that the existing steamer would be renamed TS *Queen Mary II*, and in 1934 the new liner was launched with the royal prayer by Queen Mary as RMS *Queen Mary*. She was to distinguish herself during the Second World War in her contribution to the liberty of the free nations by transporting a total of nearly 800,000 troops to numerous theatres of war around the globe, successfully avoiding aerial attack, surface and submarine attack largely by means of her Blue Riband speed.

In December 1942, the *Queen Mary* was carrying exactly 16,082 American troops from New York to Great Britain, the most ever transported aboard a vessel in a single voyage, when 700 miles from Scotland during a gale, she was suddenly hit broadside by a rogue wave that may have reached a height of 92 feet. An account of this incident is retained in Walter Ford Carter's book, *No Greater Sacrifice, No Greater Love*. Carter's father, Dr Norval Carter, part of the 110th Station Hospital on board at the time, wrote that at one point *Queen Mary* 'damned near capsized ... One moment the top deck was at its usual height and then, swoom! Down, over, and forward she would pitch'. The incident inspired Paul Gallico's book, *The Poseidon Adventure*, which was later made into a film using the *Queen Mary* as a stand-in for the SS *Poseidon*.

During the Second World War, RMS *Queen Mary* carried British Prime Minister Winston Churchill across the Atlantic for meetings with fellow Allied forces officials. He would be listed on the passenger manifest as 'Colonel Warden' but insisted that the lifeboat assigned to him had a .303 machine gun fitted to it so he could 'resist capture at all costs'. As it happened this was no idle threat. Action had to be taken when the *Queen Mary* was in South American waters, a radio signal having been intercepted which indicated that spies had reported her last refuelling stop and a U-boat was waiting on her line of voyage. After being alerted, the *Queen Mary* took evasive action to avoid the intended U-boat interception.

After the war, in 1951, Anthony Blunt (of the Cambridge ring of spies, whose combined activities betrayed numerous secrets to Stalin including details of the atom bomb) met his friend and co-spy Guy Burgess at Southampton Royal Ocean Terminal. Blunt's Soviet controller, Yuri Modin, recollected that the only way to secure Maclean's vanishing to Moscow was for Burgess to accompany him. Maclean was in London but Burgess in America: 'They knew they were caught in a race against time – and they also knew that the *Queen Mary* would take at least five days to carry Burgess across the Atlantic.'[9] Blunt met Burgess, at Philby's instruction, to tip off Maclean that the latter was exposed by a cryptographer who identified his codename 'Homer' on 30 March 1951 while working on the top secret Venona transcripts, and he would have to defect immediately and sneak away from duties in the London Foreign Office to journey to Moscow at the earliest opportunity. Yet there is suggestion that RMS *Queen Mary* may have harboured a greater secret and been the innocent means by which Anthony Blunt also sent warning to Burgess in Washington of Maclean's imminent exposure without the Venona transcripts as the origin. Blunt may have encoded in a special copy of his book *The Nation's Treasures* the need for Maclean to flee by means of rendezvous with Burgess upon the latter's return from America. This book was sent to Burgess via an old boyfriend of Blunt, Alan Baker, who was visiting Washington not long before Burgess returned from America. Blunt did much the same using a print of Piranesi's *Antonine Column* sent via the Soviet diplomatic bag from Kensington to Moscow to relay a message to Philby in Moscow immediately following Blunt's exposure by Margaret Thatcher in the House of Commons in 1979. If so, then it means that there was a very important and senior spy in the upper echelons of British Intelligence as yet unexposed – someone who had knowledge of Venona.

Ironically, Anthony Blunt's mother had been a childhood friend of Queen Mary, and he claimed distant kinship with Queen Elizabeth being her third cousin through their common ancestor, George Smith, MP for Selsdon in 1792.

RMS *Queen Mary* is now preserved at Long Beach, California, though her sister ship, RMS *Queen Elizabeth*, launched on the Clyde in 1938 by the late Queen Elizabeth the Queen Mother, and equally loved and renowned for her wartime and post-war career, sustained a crippling fire in 1982 in Hong Kong Harbour following her conversion to become *Seawise University*. The fire prevented any chance of preservation and gave her a crazy list. Nevertheless before scrapping she earned a place in that sad condition in a James Bond film as a secret headquarters of MI6, crewed by 'Q', 'M', Miss Moneypenny and others of the Royal Navy. As it happens she was entitled to fly the Blue Ensign when at sea as her Captain was always required to be of Royal Naval Reserve status in case of Naval Control Shipping 'take-up'.

There was neither royal prayer nor ceremonial breaking of a bottle on *Titanic*'s bows at her launch on 31 May 1911, but rather a signal was given by Lord Pirrie, Chairman of Harland & Wolff, for the firing of rockets. It took 62 seconds for *Titanic*'s hull – over 882 feet long and weighing 24,360 tons – to slide from her building berth into the waters of Belfast harbour. Through the courtesy of the Harbour Commissioners, the Albert Quay was reserved to the authorities of two excellent charities, the Children's Hospital in Queen Street and the Ulster Hospital for Children and Women, and a charge was made for admission, the object being to benefit the two institutions named. The ceremony had been fixed for a 12.15 p.m., and ten minutes before that time a red flag was hoisted at the stern of the vessel. Five minutes later two rockets were discharged, shortly afterwards the explosion of another rocket was heard, and at 12.13 p.m. the spectators had the joy and satisfaction of seeing the vessel in motion.

Rockets were to play a central role in her life. Despite the impending tragedy that was to befall the vessel at the mercy of an iceberg in the North Atlantic on 14 April 1912, when rockets in the night sky from the approaching *Californian* were the last thing to be observed by many from the decks of the sinking ship, some lasting benefit flowed from the generosity of the charitable contributions made at her launch. The author's family papers contain correspondence of a relative[10] (who attended the inquiry into her loss) that refers to the 1962 deathbed confession of the Chief Officer of a sailing barque, *Samson*, who admitted that he had seen the *Titanic*'s distress flares but dared not approach to assist as he was illegally fishing for seals, using a nearby iceberg as a fridge. The lights of the *Samson* were mistaken by some survivors for those of the more distant *Californian* whose Captain was instead blamed for tardiness in assisting. This evidence has hitherto never been satisfactorily examined.

A long-term benefit to all mariners nevertheless arose from the official enquiry into this maritime disaster. This was the founding of the London Nautical School, now situated on the South Bank of the River Thames, but originally established as a Nautical Department of the Rotherhithe New Road (Higher Grade) School in 1915. The objectives of the Nautical Department were to 'to educate and prepare cadets to be able to meet the needs of society, either at sea or in any other occupation, where responsibility, attention to duty and regard for others are valued equally with academic and practical skills'. The school is affiliated to HMS *Richmond*, a Type 23 Duke Class Anti-Submarine Warfare Frigate, and the cadets participate annually at the Service for Seafarers at St Paul's Cathedral, finding a contingent of boys also to attend the annual Merchant Naval Service of Remembrance at Tower Hill.

Royal prayer at ship launching is common to other modern monarchies. For instance, with the Dutch monarchy, Queen Beatrix recently launched the largest ship ever to fly the Dutch flag, MS *Eurodam*. Of the 135-year-old Holland America Line, nine vessels have been launched by members of the Dutch royal family, including the *Statendam III* in 1929 by Prince Hendrik; *Nieuw Amsterdam* in 1937 by Queen Wilhelmina; *Statendam IV* in 1957 and *Prinses Margriet* in 1964 by then Princess Beatrix; *Rotterdam V* in 1958 by Queen Juliana; and *Prinsendam* in 1973, *Nieuw Amsterdam* in 1983, *Rotterdam VI* in 1997 and *Oosterdam* in 2003 by Princess Margriet.

On 10 March 2008, Queen Sophia of Spain launched the largest ship in the Spanish navy, named after her husband, the aircraft carrier *Juan Carlos I*, at Ferrol at 6.09 p.m. to coincide with the high tide.

Notes

[1] The Christian 'Nestorian Monument' testifying to their introduction of the 'Illustrious Religion' in the Middle Kingdom of China was erected on 4th February AD 781 40 miles south-west of Sianfu in the sub-prefecture of Chowchih. One of the inscriptions is in T'ang dynasty calligraphy and the other is in Syriac. It was discovered by Jesuit missionaries to China in 1624. Christianity had enjoyed the patronage of several Chinese emperors, beginning with the mission of the Nestorian monk, O-lo-pen, to the capital in AD 635. Li Chih-tsao published an account of the monument as early as 1625, and Manoel Dias wrote a scholarly description of it, published under the title 'Ching-chiao pei-ch'an' at Hangchow in 1644.

[2] Author retains a photographic collection following inspection of the Warship rings at the Museo Historico Navale, Venice, with kind permission of the Italian Navy.

[3] Renowned not only as strategic Royal Navy base for the Allied war effort during two world wars (The Falklands saw major battles within sight of its islands in both world wars, the Royal Navy even retiring to Port Stanley for repairs and re-victualling following the Battle of the River Plate), many of the Falkland Islands' structures were simply an extension of Britain itself. Even the Camber narrow-gauge steam railway was manufactured and shipped to the Falklands during the

First World War to move coal and other supplies for the Royal Navy between Camber Depot at Navy Point (opposite Port Stanley) to Moody Brook Marine Base to transport coal in sufficient quantities to fuel the steam generator that powered the new invention of a giant 'spark transmitter' for sending signals between the Falklands and the Great Britain. So effective was the invention that its signals were noticed by a United States warship in the North Sea during its testing. The two Kerr Stuart saddle tank locomotives, built in 1915, survived in use until the mid-1920s when they were dumped into the harbour, only to be rescued decades later by the Royal Engineers and stored there pending eventual restoration. Among the unusual examples of rolling stock employed on the 3.5 mile line were manned sail-powered wagons, and on 28 February 2005 old photographs of the railway in use were incorporated into a special issue of postage stamps, one even capturing 'Falklands Islands Express' written on the side of a train.

[4] The submission from the Chiefs of Staff to the Cabinet's Overseas Policy and Defence Committee in the last of three meetings in November 1977 saw the necessity to deploy two Frigates in the mid-Atlantic immediately for communications purposes, while the 'Fleet submarine could, on the other hand, be deployed close to the Islands on a covert basis' (interview with Ted Rowlands in *The Times*, 15 January 1983, supplemented and corrected by Dr David Owen). In the event the Prime Minister used his own Second World War Royal Navy experience to devise the strategy. He ordered HMS *Dreadnought* to break surface and be seen close to the Islands, while two frigates (*HMS Alacrity* and HMS *Phoebe*) were indeed deployed mid-Atlantic and primed to head for the Falklands if the ploy did not work. See also newly declassified Foreign Office files at the National Archives released in January 2009 concerning the chronology of the discovery in February 1978 by the RRS *Bransfield* of the Argentine occupation of Southern Thule that had persisted since 1976 and was known to the British government. Now 'it was relevant that the RRS Bransfield had recently discovered the base in Thule and the crew might talk about this on their arrival in Port Stanley on February 20th' flashed David Owen to the British Embassy in Buenos Aires on 17 February 1978, with the inevitability of conflict as a consequence. See also E.J. Grove, *Vanguard to Trident – British Naval Policy since World War II* (London: Bodley Head, 1987), pp. 358–9. Groves was former Deputy Head of Strategic Studies at the Royal Naval College, Dartmouth.

[5] *Official Recommissioning Programme: HMS Daring*: (50 D2027) Dd. 145791 14M 2166 15 & 5. Ltd Gp 404.

2

'Near Miss' Royal Prayers

By 'Near Miss' is meant the absence of royal prayers in circumstances where they either were, or might have been, expected – but were trumped by coincidence, politics, or by deliberate or inadvertent omission.

A Couple of Bridges

The royal blessing of bridges provides a particularly rich vein of near misses. Bridges have a long association with royalty. St Edmund, the English king who in 869 was defeated by the Danes, made hiding from them under the arches of a bridge his choice of refuge. Thereafter bridge chapels were often dedicated to him, including one in Exeter, now a ruin beside an old bridge over the Exe, and the dedication to St Edmund of the parish church at Kingsbridge in Devon is an extension of the same association.

> 'I hope God will protect all passengers By Night and By Day.'
> (Prayed by the poet William McGonagall in the absence of The Queen at the opening of the Tay Railway Bridge)

In the case of the Tay Bridge in Scotland spanning the Firth of Tay between Dundee and Wormit, Queen Victoria gave Royal Assent to the North British Railway (Tay Bridge) Act on 22 July 1871,[1] but was unable to open it. She did, however, knight its designer, Thomas Bouch, who employed the lattice-grid design combining wrought and cast iron, first used by Kennard for the Crumlin Viaduct in South Wales in 1858.[2]

The spectacular use of cast iron in the building of the Crystal Palace encouraged Bouch to emulate the success of the cast-iron girder construction he saw Gustave Eiffel using in 1867 for his large viaducts in the Massif Central. All manner of notables visited the structure while it was under construction, including Ulysses S. Grant who commented that 'it was a big bridge for a small city'. Charles Cowan, director of Bouch's Penicuik river-hugging railway, recorded his own accompanying of Ulysses Grant on 1 September 1877 by train from Burntisland to Tayport and then their own viewing of the structure from a steam boat below, together with a visit to the juvenile young offenders' old wooden training warship *Mars*: 'I sat opposite General Grant, and we had some conversation on the connection of his ancestors with Scotland, which dates from about two hundred years ago, he having sprung, I believe, from the Grants of Seafield, the Head of whom is the Earl of Strathspey ...'. The first engine to cross was on 22 September 1877 and the North British Railway opened it on 1 June 1878.

William Topaz McGonagall's famous poem 'The Railway Bridge of the Silvery Tay' contains in the fifth verse the line 'I hope God will protect all passengers By night and by Day'. It was a prayer that the Sovereign would undoubtedly have expressed in much the same terms had she actually opened the bridge, as averred erroneously by many histories that she did. Queen Victoria did cross the bridge, but in the summer of the next year as her diary entry of 20 June 1879 records:

> We reached the Tay Bridge station at six. Immense crowds everywhere, flags waving in every direction, the whole population out; but one's heart was too sad for anything. The Provost, splendidly attired, presented an address. Ladies presented beautiful bouquets to Beatrice and me. The last time I was in Dundee was in September 1844, just after Affie's birth, when we landed there on our way to Blair, and Vicky, then not four years old, the only child with us was carried through the crowd by old Renwick. We embarked there also on our way back. We stopped here about five minutes, and then began going over the marvellous Tay Bridge, which is rather more than a mile and a half long. It was begun in 1871. There were great difficulties in laying the foundation, and some lives were lost. It was finished in 1878. Mr. Bouch, who was presented at Dundee, was the engineer. It took us, I should say, about eight minutes going over. The view was very fine.[3]

Queen Victoria Crossing Tay Bridge. Original image published by Illustrated London News, issue of 5 July 1879. ILN Picture Library Code: ILNG001123

There was an *Illustrated London News* engraving of Queen Victoria leaning out of her carriage window as she crossed the bridge on 20 June 1879, taking the opportunity to observe the complement of her training ship *Mars* moored below in the Tay estuary.

But disaster was to strike only five months later on Sunday 28 December 1879 at 7.15 p.m. with the Night Mail crossing: 'A trail of fire and a sudden shower of sparks seen for a moment from the shore were the sole signal made by the train as it shot with a multitude of human beings into the abyss below' (*The Times*, 30 December 1879). There were no survivors and of the 75 occupants of the train only 46 bodies were ever recovered, the number of passengers and crew being determined by close examination of tickets issued from as far as King's Cross.

Many reasons have been advanced for the collapse of the

Tay Bridge Disaster illustrated in Christian Herald, issue of Wednesday, 7 January 1880

central section of the bridge. The Board of Inquiry chaired by the Commissioner of Wrecks, concluded that the bridge was 'badly designed, badly built, and badly maintained, and that its downfall was due to inherent defects in the structure, which must sooner of later have brought it down'.[4] Bouch was made a scapegoat and died a disconsolate man, but there may have been more to it than wind pressure, measured that night by HMS *Mars* as force 10 to 11 with gusts even higher, the full moon being obscured by cloud, for which crosswinds Bouch had not calculated in his design, blowing the train off the rails or bringing down the bridge, or else faulty materials compounded by ill-fitting 'chattering' joints that eventually gave way under the weight of the train.

While it is certain that Queen Victoria was spared disaster on her earlier journey across the Tay Bridge – there was subsequent persistent conjecture throughout the late nineteenth century in the Dundee community that Karl Marx intended to travel from Edinburgh, where he had been staying over Christmas, to friends in the North by the very night train that plummeted into the Tay. He is said to have escaped this fate through catching a cold and saying put instead. There were also differing recollections between witnesses to the Board of Inquiry over what happened that night. The Board Report chose to let one represent all – the evidence of a North British railway employee, John Watt, who was in the bridge cabin at the south end when the train passed:

> According to Watt, when the train had gone two hundred yards from the cabin, he observed sparks flying from the wheels, and after they had continued about three minutes, there was a sudden bright flash of light, and in an instant there was total darkness, the tail lamps of the train, the sparks, the flash of light, all he said disappearing in an instant.

The possibility of a sinister motive was not considered by the inquiry. A hundred years later in 1979, the Surveyor Emeritus of the Queen's Pictures, Sir Anthony Blunt, was exposed to Parliament as a spy by Prime Minister Margaret Thatcher. Ironically, among one of the papers Blunt had retrieved on the King's secret mission to the Schloss Friedrichshoff at the close of the Second World War was a letter written by Karl Marx, who had been called upon by a German court official in 1847. It was in 1847 that Marx had been asked to write a political programme for the Communist League – the result of the joint effort with Engels being the *Communist Manifesto*, the first edition coming from a publisher in Bishopsgate at 46 Liverpool Street, then very much a backwater of the City of London.[5]

Title Page of first edition of the Communist Manifesto, Karl Marx and Friederich Engels, February 1848. British Library acquisition 2009

For Marx, religion, and therefore royal prayer, was a sham to palliate the downtrodden, summed up as 'opiate of the people', and monarchy a passing anachronism of the old order of society. Marxism was to supply the philosophy behind the creation of the Union of Soviet Socialist Republics (USSR) in 1917, and to spread to China under the Maoist Chairmanship and elsewhere. The quotation 'Die Religion … ist das Opium des Volkes' (i.e. 'Religion … is the opiate of the masses') in its original German wording came from Marx's own Introduction to his 1843 work entitled 'A Contribution to the Critique of Hegel's Philosophy of

Right', released in February 1844 in Marx and Arnold Ruge's journal, *Deutsch-Französische Jahrbücher.*[6]

When revolution broke out in 1848, the Prussian King dissolved the Assembly and Marx was taken to court. He argued that the King's actions were illegal and that armed resistance was justified. Although he was acquitted unanimously, he was expelled from Prussia in 1849 and returned to London. Had any authority wished to eliminate him by 1879? Certainly he was regarded as a dangerous subversive in many quarters by then, but nothing has come to light in support of the contemporary rumours in Dundee of his intention to catch the train that fell victim to the Tay Bridge disaster.

The memory of those who lost their lives was not lost within the royal family, and 'Tay Bridge' was chosen as the password for the funeral of the late Queen Elizabeth the Queen Mother.

Sydney Harbour Bridge

I open this bridge in the name of His Majesty the King and all the decent citizens of New South Wales. (Not uttered, as intended, by John Lang, Premier of New South Wales)

The Sydney Harbour Bridge was opened on 19 March 1932 after eight years of construction neither by King George V, nor the Premier of New South Wales in his stead in the presence of the Governor Sir Philip Game (who ended up reading a congratulatory message from King George V during the proceedings), but by an unexpected hand. Two days before the opening, the Premier of New South Wales, John Lang, whom it was decided would officially open the bridge, received an urgent telegram from his agent in London, Mr A.C. Willis. Some members of the House of Commons claimed to have received reliable information of a plot in Sydney to have Mr Lang thrown 172 feet over the side of the bridge into the sea during the opening ceremony. Extensive security precautions were put in place with mounted and pedestrian police in phalanxes, but as the 21-gun salute began and the band struck up 'Advance, Australia Fair!' a man on a chestnut horse, dressed in military uniform, strode forward

Colonel Dr Groot cutting the Sydney Harbour Bridge Ribbon. New South Wales State Archives

through the police ranks, outflanked Mr Lang who was about to cut the ribbon, drew his ceremonial sword and cut the ribbon himself, at the same time declaring 'I open this bridge in the name of His Majesty the King and all the decent citizens of New South Wales'.

He was subsequently dragged from his horse, had his ceremonial sword confiscated and was fined £5 for trespassing.[7] De Groot turned out to be a Hussar and entitled to carry a sword but had joined the 'New Guard' – a 'fascist' movement that did not see eye to eye with the left-wing politics of Mr Lang. The Mayor of North Sydney at the other end of the bridge, Alderman Primrose, experienced no such disruptions, but turned out, conveniently, also to be member of the 'New Guard'.

But everything de Groot did was legal. He claimed that he was insulted that neither a member of the royal family nor the Governor-General had opened the bridge and argued successfully in the Supreme Court against the charge of 'insulting behaviour' since that charge could only apply to public places. If the bridge was private the charge would necessarily be dropped, but could only stand if public. But if public, then De Groot argued again successfully that since the bridge was part of the King's highway he had the right under common law to clear it of any obstruction that impeded its use, including ribbon strung across it. His sword was also returned to him in an out-of-court settlement when he sued for wrongful arrest on the grounds that the policeman had no grounds to arrest a soldier. De Groot took his sword back to his family farm in County Wicklow, Ireland, from where it emerged eventually, at his wish, to be returned to Australia. Its whereabouts remained unknown until the deliverer of a lecture in Dublin in 2004 raised the question of its whereabouts, only to be told by de Groot's nephew, who happened to be in the audience, that he possessed it! Part of the ribbon cut by De Groot's sword survives in the Power House Collection, Sydney.

King George V had in fact, along with Queen Mary, opened Sydney Harbour Bridge's 'little brother' in England, the New Tyne Bridge at Newcastle, on 10 October 1928. To commemorate the event the King gave a cheque for underprivileged children to have a day out to the coast – perpetuated as the 'Sunshine Fund'.

The Millennium Bridge

The iconic and immediately much loved new 'Millennium Bridge', designed by Wilkinson Eyre and Gifford, was built by Volker Stevin. Known locally as the 'Winking Eye Bridge' from its looks, it spans the River Tyne between Gateshead and Newcastle as a pedestrian and cyclist tilt bridge. It was lifted into place as a single structure by one of the world's largest floating cranes (Asian Hercules) on 20 November 2000. Open to the public on 17 September 2001, the bridge was dedicated by The Queen on 7 May 2002.

However, the London Millennium Bridge – more commonly known as the 'Wobbly Bridge' – has had a far more eventful life. Its origin lay in the 1996 *Financial Times* competition launched in conjunction with the Royal Institute of British Architects and the London Borough of Southwark for the first footbridge to span the river since Tower Bridge in 1894. It was to connect Blackfriars and St Paul's Cathedral on the North Bank with the Tate Modern and the Globe on the South Bank. It earns a mention because The Queen ended up opening a bridge which was then closed.

The Queen, accompanied by the Duke of Edinburgh, the Bishop of London and the Lord Mayor, opened it on Tuesday 9 May 2000 (before its completion and eventual opening on 10 June 2000) with the following words of dedication: 'I dedicate this Bridge as a symbol of the new millennium to the people of Southwark and of the City of London and to all who shall pass over it from all over the world.' This dedication was preceded by a Blessing from the Bishop of London.

Opened to the public on 10 June with 90,000 people crossing on its first day, it immediately became something of a 'white knuckle' ride owing to its unforeseen swaying motion. Now known as 'synchronous lateral excitation', the bridge took on a life of its own and swayed 70 mm from side to side as people crossed it. Attempts to limit the numbers crossing led to huge queues and it was closed two days later, reopening in February with the problem solved. Other bridges, such as the Auckland Harbour Road Bridge in New Zealand filmed swaying during a demonstration in 1975, are known to suffer from the same phenomenon. The Millennium Bridge is an exposed structure and the police took action to close it for the duration of 'Storm Kyrill' on 18 January 2007 in order that nobody found themselves blown off it into the river. It features in the film *Harry Potter and the Half Blood Prince* falling into the river at the behest of Voldemort.

Notes

[1] Dundee University Archive: MS 17/2 Thornton College of Plans and Manuscripts, 1846–1902, papers and correspondence relating to the Tay Bridge Enquiry and Tay Bridge Bill, 1869–88.
[2] Dundee University Archive: MS 30 Tay Bridge Collection, 1979. Display material used in commemorative exhibition December/January 1979/1980, of the centenary of the Tay Bridge Disaster and

marks the career of Sir Thomas Bouch, engineer of the first Tay Bridge. Includes mounted photocopies, drawings, articles and prints about the old and new Tay Bridges, and a diagram showing design of Tay Bridge, with original design also indicated, etc.

3 There are a total of 111 manuscript volumes of *Queen Victoria's Diary* in the Royal Archives at Windsor Castle, mostly in Princess Beatrice's hand because Queen Victoria requested her youngest daughter to edit them upon her death and she destroyed most of the original entries after transcribing them.

4 *Court of Inquiry Report*, National Archives: Rail 1014/37/8/64, and *Report of Court of Enquiry, and of Mr Rothery, upon the circumstances attending the fall of a portion of the Tay Bridge on 28th December 1879*, National Archives: ZHC/1/4258. Also Parliamentary Archives: *Tay Bridge Disaster Report of the Board of Inquiry and report of Mr Rothery upon the circumstances attending the fall of a portion of the Tay Bridge on 28th December 1879, presented to both Houses of Parliament by Command of Her Majesty* (London: HMSO, 1880), p. 9.

5 Karl Marx and Frederick Engels, *Manifest der Kommunistischen Partei* (London: D.C. Burghard, 1848), British Library Reading Room. The first edition of 1848 was acquired by the BL in 2009 and is the only copy in the world to be available in a national library.

6 In this Marx elaborated further, venturing that: 'Religion is the general theory of this world ... and its universal basis of consolation and justification ... The struggle against religion is, therefore, indirectly the struggle against that world whose spiritual aroma is religion ... Religion is the sigh of the oppressed creature, the heart of a heartless world, and the soul of soulless conditions. It is the opium of the people. The abolition of religion as the illusory happiness of the people is the demand for their happiness. To call on them to give up their illusions about their condition is to call on them to give up a condition that requires illusions. The criticism of religion is, therefore, in embryo, the criticism of that vale of tears of which religion is the halo.'

7 Sequence of four sequential photographs by anonymous cameraman capturing 'The De Groot Incident', University of Sydney Library, 1932.

3

The Modern Application of Some Old Royal Prayers

The legacy of the Reformation in the sixteenth century was to influence the means by which provision could be made for those members of the royal family who professed Roman Catholicism. The matter was brought to a head, albeit unwittingly, with the importation of Roman Catholicism occasioned by royal marriage to a princess of Roman Catholic persuasion. Later, in the seventeenth century, the provision for royal prayer in a royal marriage service became intertwined with the matter of national defence, as it provided the excuse and means by which another mutually advantageous formal diplomatic treaty could be undertaken between England and Portugal.

The building of the Queen's Chapel at St James's Palace was thus begun in 1623 specifically for the Roman Catholic worship requirements of the intended consort to Prince Charles. It was initially established by the Anglo-Spanish Treaty of 1623 signed in the Church of England Chapel Royal at Whitehall by the Spanish Ambassador and King James I, with the Dean of the Chapel Royal overseeing the swearing of the necessary oaths. This created the Roman Catholic enclaves of the two Queen's Chapels at St James's Palace and Somerset House.

This 1623 Anglo-Spanish Treaty was superseded by the 1625 Anglo-French Treaty, with Henrietta Maria of France[1] eventually becoming Charles's bride, and the Queen's Chapel was completed for her use by 1626 in accordance with the specific provisions of that treaty.

Despite the regicide of Charles I in 1649, and Charles II's exile in France, a defence pact with Portugal was reaffirmed by

Cromwell in 1654. With the return from exile of Charles II and the Restoration of the Monarchy in 1660, King Charles II determined to marry Catharine of Braganza.

The Anglo-Portuguese Treaty of 1661 turned out to be a combined marriage and defence treaty.[2] The marriage element is found at Section VII which reads: 'It is also agreed, that Her Majesty and whole Family shall enjoy the free exercise of the Roman Catholic religion, and to that purpose shall have a Chapel, or some other place set apart for the exercise thereof . . . ' The upshot of this provision was the renovation and use of the Queen's Chapel at St James's Palace for Roman Catholic worship from 1661 by such members of the royal family who professed it.

Since the treaty provision had no end-date, and referred not only to the Queen but also to the 'whole Family', it was invoked after Charles II's death by James II to permit Mary of Modena, his wife, to receive Roman Catholic services there after 1685. Roman Catholic services at the Queen's Chapel were ended by William of Orange following his successful invasion in 1688, actually against the terms of the 1661 Treaty, not least because Catherine of Braganza continued to reside in Britain. The actuality became that from 1688 the Queen's Chapel was given over to Reform Church worship within the royal household and found itself hosting French, German, Dutch and Danish Lutheran worshipping Court congregations and ministers, though all such ministers had to be approved by the Dean of the Chapel Royal.

The use of the Queen's Chapel was given over entirely by King George VI to the Chapel Royal as late as 1938, but the use of the chapel is still subject to the Anglo-Portuguese Treaty of 1661, and the present situation is unique in the UK. The use of the Queen's Chapel is in effect held in trust by the Sovereign for application in accordance with the provisions and legacy of the Anglo-Portuguese Treaty as the Sovereign sees fit to apply it. Thus any royal member of the 'whole Family' can be granted the privilege of receiving Roman Catholic ministration there if the Sovereign were to so permit and facilitate in accordance with Article VII of the 1661 Treaty.

The 1661 Marriage Treaty Secret Article concludes:

It is by this Secret Article concluded and accorded that His Majesty of Great Britain, in regard of the great advantages and increase of Dominion he hath purchased by the above-mentioned Treaty of Marriage, shall promise and oblige himself, as by this present Article he doth, to defend and protect all Conquests and Colonies belonging to the Crown of Portugal, against all his enemies, as well future as present.

The treaty also, directly by Article XV, required one country to bind itself for the future to defend the other against invasion. This reaffirmed the 1373 and 1386 Treaties of Alliance, and was repeated in the 1661 Marriage Treaty because the original Windsor Treaty Roll could not be found at that time. It came to light later, but all remembered its provisions! The 1373 Treaty of Alliance actually stated:

In the first place we settle and covenant that there shall be from this day forward ... true, faithful, constant mutual and perpetual friendships, unions, alliances and needs of sincere affection, and that as true and faithful friends we shall henceforth, reciprocally, be friends to friends, and enemies to enemies, and shall assist maintain, and uphold each other mutually, by sea and by land, against all men that may live and die.

That the 1661 Marriage Treaty, which further elaborated upon these provisions, was still active was confirmed by it being invoked by Britain in 1700 when France declared war on Britain and demanded that Portugal close its borders to Britain. Portugal responded to the treaty provisions by joining Britain in the 'Grand Alliance' against France in 1703, as requested by John Methuen, Britain's official emissary to Portugal, in accordance with the 1661 Anglo-Portuguese Treaty. The Methuen Treaty of 1703 reaffirmed the earlier treaty provisions. When Napoleon marched into Lisbon in 1807 the Portuguese royal family fled to Brazil and invoked the 1386 Treaty of Windsor (which had increased the mutual defence provisions of the 1373 Treaty) and its successors. British generals Beresford and Wellington conducted the Iberian Peninsula War in response and defeated Napoleon three years later. As a result Britain was permitted direct trading rights with Brazil.

That the 1661 terms were still deemed critical to the defence of Britain and Portugal was confirmed by the 1899 secret declaration, signed and hosted by the Foreign Office, reaffirming all the Anglo-Portuguese ancient treaties of alliance. The 1661 Anglo-Portuguese Marriage Treaty and other earlier treaties were all recognized in the Treaties of Arbitration between Britain and Portugal in 1904 and 1914, either side of the overthrow of the Portuguese monarchy in 1910.

More spectacularly, the 1661 Marriage Treaty was invoked in the Second World War initially to require Portugal to remain neutral despite German pressure, and was fully invoked by Churchill in 1943 to require Portugal to offer aerodrome and nautical facilities at Terceira in the Portuguese islands of the Azores to operate Royal Navy anti-U-boat operations.[3]

More recently it was invoked during the 1982 Falklands War to permit airborne and naval operations in the South Atlantic to include facilities in the Azores off the North African coast.

It has also been invoked to permit the hosting of meetings in the Azores between the Prime Ministers of the UK, Portugal and Spain, and the President of the United States of America in 2003 as prelude to the Second Gulf War, and remains active today in war theatres in Iraq and Afghanistan.

Notes

[1] The original Anglo-French Marriage Treaty of 1625 is in the Royal Archives at Windsor Castle.

[2] The 'Treaty between Great Britain and Portugal, signed at Whitehall 23rd June 1661' is reprinted in Clive Parry (ed.), *The Consolidated Treaty Series*, vol. VI, 1660–61 (Dobbs Ferry, NY: Oceana Publications, 1969–81), from British & Foreign State Papers, vol. I, p. 494. A Portuguese version is found in Collecção dos Tratados, vol. I, p. 234.

[3] Winston Churchill, *Closing the Ring* (New York: Houghton Mifflin, 1951).

4

Royal Prayers in Scotland

The English Chapel Royal was to play an important role in the origin of discontent that has led to the present constitutional obligation of the Sovereign, taken at the Accession Council at the beginning of each new reign, to protect the Church of Scotland.

Central to the present existence of this other Established Church within the United Kingdom was the figure of the mysterious John Knox. He was born about 1515 but nothing is known of his family origins save that his mother was a Sinclair – and in all probability therefore he was descended from the Earls of Orkney. There is no contemporary record of his having graduated at any university, though both Glasgow and St Andrew's claim him as an alumnus. Most of the 'facts' surrounding his early life come from his own memoirs. These, though, are full of inaccuracies and hyperbole. His service as a galley slave followed his incarceration in St Andrew's Castle for overtly lauding the murder of Cardinal Beaton in revenge for the murder of the protestant preacher George Wishart. The French Fleet arrived to reinforce a siege of the Castle and on 31 July 1547, the Castle was surrendered, and Knox was taken prisoner, forcibly drafted for service aboard French galleys and was later imprisoned at Rouen. But in 1549 Knox was freed and chose to go to England to serve the Court of the Protestant King Edward VI.

As Yeoman of the Vestry, an officer subject to the authority of the Serjeant of the Vestry of the English Chapel Royal in 1553 under Edward VI, John Knox operated in the palaces of Whitehall and St James's.[1] He was dismissed his post under Queen Mary Tudor for not renouncing Protestantism. And so this John Knox, formerly a priest in the Roman Catholic Church, became familiar with the practices of the Church of England. After an eventful sojourn abroad in Dieppe in 1554, and then Geneva, before returning to Scotland from Dieppe to Leith by ship, landing on 2 May 1559, Knox was the recipient of money following an appeal to Queen Elizabeth. The growing Presbyterian congregation in Scotland sent Knox on a mission to secure the support of Cecil, to whom had written in 1558 with a letter for Queen Elizabeth apologizing for his earlier outburst against her relations (i.e. his 'First Blast of the Trumpet against the Monstrous Regiment of Women', which was critical of Mary Tudor, Mary of Guise, and Mary Stuart who had just married the French Dauphin). Knox sailed from Fife to Northumberland early in August 1559 and secured an interview with the Governor of Berwick, finally bringing back to Stirling letters from Cecil that seemed favourable to the congregation's appeal for help, but which were fuzzy in their commitment. Queen Elizabeth's agent, Sadler, brought the money in the hope that Knox would foment religious unrest to destabilize Catholic political machinations and the presence of French troops in Scotland – both being perceived as a threat to Elizabeth's Crown across the border in England.

But Knox departed from his brief, and added repudiation of the Church of England to his earlier dismissal of Roman Catholicism, and developed instead a form of genuine Presbyterian churchmanship which was to take Scotland by storm, and end in the unexpected and sudden demise of the authority of the English Chapel Royal in Scotland. By July 1560 the Treaty of Edinburgh was signed by representatives of England and France, providing for the withdrawal from Scottish soil of both French and English troops. The congregation held a solemn thanksgiving service at St Giles's and Parliament met on 1 August and rose on 25 August, having commissioned Knox and three other ministers to draw up the plan of church-government.

The result by 20 December 1560 was 'First Book of Discipline' and this oversaw the first meeting of the newly constituted 'General Assembly' of the Kirk. The 'Book of Discipline' was based largely upon the Genevan *Ordonnances* and upon the formularies of the German Church founded in London in 1550, and markedly Calvinist. Thus was born the Church of Scotland as a national entity.

Although Knox died in 1572, his legacy challenged the incautious desire of the Dean of the Chapel Royal, William Laud, Dean of the English Chapel Royal 1626–33, to impose in Scotland the music and liturgy of the English Chapel Royal. The director of music of the Scottish Chapel Royal, Edward Kelly, was ordered to London in 1630. In London Kelly took five months to copy out 'twelve great books, gilded, and twelve small ones with an organ book', also engaging an organist, 'two men for playing on the cornets and sackbuts, and two boys for singing divisions in the verses'. By 1631/32 Kelly was able to report that Holyrood Palace was now serviced by 16 men, six boys and an organist. The men sang in black gowns and the boys in 'sad coloured coats'. Laud tightened up Court attendance and required members of the Scottish Council and other departments of state to attend communion at Holyrood Palace – with the communion being conducted to the sounds of trumpets at the King's command. This was the situation on the eve of the arrival in Edinburgh, after a journey by land via Durham, of Charles I in preparation for his coronation as King of Scotland in 1633.

He was to be joined by the English Chapel Royal who had meanwhile sailed up the North Sea aboard the *Dreadnought*.[2] This was an old warship that had undergone rebuilding since distinguishing herself in the capture of the *San Felipe* in 1587 upon returning from 'singing the King of Spain's beard' in the Cadiz raid. It was the discovery of papers aboard the *San Felipe* revealing the enormous profits the Spanish were making from the East Indies that led directly to the foundation of the East India Company of London. Also an old veteran of the Spanish Armada in 1588, having taken part in action off Lyme Regis, Dunnose Point in the Isle of Wight and Gravelines, in 1633 *Dreadnought* now sailed up the Firth of Forth, in company with the *Blessing of Burt Island*, but which latter vessel had the misfortune to capsize with loss of life and Charles I's silver dinner service. It remains on site beneath the sea off Edinburgh.

Many Scots remained unimpressed and entertained suspicions about the intentions of the King in imposing the pomp and ceremony of the English Chapel Royal – suspicions confirmed by the King's command within two months of his return to London that services be conducted by the Scottish Chapel Royal twice daily 'with the choir, as well in our absence as otherwise'. Then William Laud was elevated from Dean of the Chapel Royal to become Archbishop of Canterbury. The final straw occurred with the attempted imposition of a 'Revised Prayer Book' for Scotland, which was read for the first time at St Giles's Church in Edinburgh on 23 July 1637. The reaction was violent, with the Scottish Privy Council being forced to take refuge in Holyrood Palace while the public rioted and desecrated Holyrood Chapel, the minister for Kilwinning, Robert Baillie, noting that 'Almost all our nobility and gentry of both sexes count that book little better than the Mass'. How right he was, for on 28 February 1638 the 'National Covenant' was signed declaring that the King's church reforms 'tend to the re-establishment of the popish religion and tyranny, and to the subversion of the true reformed religion, and of our liberties, laws and estates'. The King raised an army to face down 'this small cloud in the North', but Civil War broke out in England and the Parliamentarians secured the support of an increasing number of Scottish Covenanters by means of the 'Solemn League and Covenant' signed in 1643. Even after his surrender to the Scottish forces at Newark in May 1646, Charles I refused terms the Covenanters offered to secure his release while incarcerated in Carisbrooke Castle on the Isle of Wight, thus securing for himself the certain death he underwent at the Banqueting House in Whitehall on 30 January 1648 (Old Style) for the cause of the Church of England.

With the end of the Stuart tenure of the thrones of Scotland and England in 1688, the question of protecting the Scottish Presbyterian inheritance became paramount, as the prospect of a Roman Catholic monarch loomed. William of Orange's invasion to prevent that potential succession led to the religious constitutional obligations laid upon the Sovereign even today.

The position of the Sovereign vis-à-vis the Church of Scotland is an extremely complicated matter, revolving around the provisions in Article XXV of the 1706 Act of Union with Scotland, and the earlier 1688 Bill of Rights, the 1688 Coronation Oath Act, the 1700 Act of Settlement and, of great significance, the Protestant Religion and Presbyterian Church (PRPC) Act of 1707 (being the only Act named in the Regency Act 1937 to which a Regent may not give assent – Section 4 as amended being still in force today), The PRPC Act of 1707 incorporates the relevant elements of the previous Acts since 1688 but, unhelpfully, assumes knowledge of those parts of the 1688 and 1690 Acts that ratified the provision that

> it shall be lawful in the kirk and ministers, every year, at least, and oftener, pro re nata, as occasion and necessity shall require, to hold and keep General Assemblies; providing that the King's Majesty, or his Commissioners with them to be appointed by His Highness, be present at each General Assembly before the dissolving thereof, nominate time and place when and where the next General Assembly shall be holden.

In other words, the session of the General Assembly can only take place legally when the Sovereign, or the Sovereign's appointed Commissioner, is present to permit it to convene. The General Assembly then proceeds to govern all its affairs without hindrance of participation of any kind by the Sovereign, or the Sovereign's Commissioner.

The Sovereign's role is purely that of protection of the existence of the Church of Scotland under the Constitution, as defined by these Acts, which are imposed in the duty of the Sovereign to swear to that effect at the Accession Council at St James's Palace as the first requirement of a new monarch, to permit the convening of each General Assembly, and subsequent withdrawal from its proceedings – though there is nothing to prevent mere attendance at the Assembly purely as an observer.

Membership of the Church of Scotland involves baptism and confirmation by the Church of Scotland, the latter profession of confirmation which their own official literature states as occurring: 'from around the age of 16, and, admits the individual to all the rights and privileges of church membership. The person's name is then added to the congregation's communion roll and they become eligible to vote in Church meetings and be elected to offices such as the eldership'. There is also a process to permit attending a different congregation when moving domicile: 'when Church members move from one congregation to another they take with them a Certificate of Transference, commonly known a "lines" '.

The Sovereign cannot be an 'ordinary member' of the Church of Scotland, for that would equip the Sovereign with rights to engage in the governing proceedings of the Church – the very activity the various Acts were constructed carefully to prohibit and dispossess the Sovereign by so doing. By definition, for an 'ordinary member' to be denied the rights of an 'ordinary member', that person cannot not an 'ordinary member'.

But Queen Victoria was not minded to recognize this distinction. She delighted her Scottish subjects by attending the services of the Church of Scotland once she had settled at Balmoral Castle. C. Kingsley in the February 1868 issue of *Frazer's Magazine* commented that Queen Victoria had bridged the gulf 'torn open by the madness of Laud and Charles I' and 'rebuked by silent acts, which are more powerful than words, the un-wisdom of those members of the Scotch aristocracy, who, looking down upon the Kirk as vulgar and democratic...have deserted it for the Scotch Episcopal Church, or even the communion with Rome'.[3]

In fact from 1873 Queen Victoria took communion at Crathie Church every autumn, and the Prince of Wales occasionally accompanied her when staying at Abergeldie. When old Crathie Church was dismantled in 1893 to make way for a new structure, Queen Victoria's daughters offered suggestions. Princess Beatrice wanted to see a tower that looked like the one at the gates at Coburg, but Princess Louise 'sketched out something which bowled over Pss B's German sort of cupola. Her design won the day' with the chosen architect, A. Marshall Mackenzie of Edinburgh, carrying out the suggestion and the church was completed in 1895. Meanwhile Queen Victoria had laid the foundation stone in September 1893 when the walls were already 3 feet high, and three of her granddaughters, Princesses Margaret, Victoria Patricia of Connaught and Victoria Eugene of

Battenberg made the libations of corn, wine and oil upon it. The whole event was painted by an Aberdonian, John Mitchell, and in 1894 his watercolour was included as an illustration within a book called *Under Lochnagar* sold to raise money for building the new church. Yet by then Queen Victoria seldom attended Crathie Church, preferring instead to have services held in Balmoral Castle.

Queen Victoria's venture across denominational borders was an early form of royal ecumenism. The present Prince of Wales has voiced his support for other denominational manifestations of Christianity, in addition to his support for the timeless 1662 Book of Common Prayer and the ancient formularies of the Church of England.

Notes

[1] National Archives, E101/427/6 f.28. Great Wardrobe Accounts relating to the funeral of King Edward VI, 8 August 1553. John Knox appears by name as Yeoman of the Vestry. Also in LC2/4 (1), ff.17a and 17b.

[2] Bodleian Library MS Rawlinson D318, fols. 41b, 42 and 42b, for Captain Sydenham's orders to sail from Deptford: 'Mr Sidenham the captaine of the shippe called the Dreadnought, where in the gentlemen of the Chappell and officers of the Vestry were with the stuff, and also the Children of the Chappell'. *Dreadnought* is depicted in the fleet at anchor in Rochester Marsh in 1633 in a huge map at Alnwick Castle, Duke of Northumberland's Collection.

[3] C. Kingsley (1868), *Frazer's Magazine*, February, pp. 166–7.

5

Royal Prayers for Bonapartes

Bogged down in a stagnating Egyptian campaign, albeit peppered with amazing discoveries by his dedicated archaeologists and artists as they gathered evidence of Egypt's classical past, and with the British having effectively destroyed his fleet in the eastern Mediterranean, Napoleon nevertheless managed to conjure up an unexpected victory at Abukir in July 1799. But it was not enough to keep him in Egypt. There is a suggestion that Sidney Smith and his fellow officers engineered the Royal Naval blockade so as to help Napoleon evade it, with the hope that he would constitute a 'royalist' element back in France to tackle increasingly republican sentiments. Whatever the truth behind this, a much more astonishing and better accredited revelation was to surface during his return voyage.

Returning by ship from Egypt together with the scientist and mathematician, Gaspard Monge, embarking at Cairo and bound for Paris in August 1799, Napoleon Bonaparte astonishingly confided to him that he could not be certain of his parentage.[1] He was aware of the rumours of an affair between Louis Charles Rene (the Comte de Marbeuf and Governor of Corsica) and Napoleon's mother, Letizia, and in front of Monge pretended to reckon the days between the Governor's departure and his own date of birth, 15 August 1769.

At Napoleon's conception it appears that Letizia was at Corte, in the Gaffori Palace. There were certainly contemporary rumours concerning the fatherhood of at least one of Letizia's children, not least those advanced by the Frenchman, the Comte de Mony-Colchen, who visited Corsica in 1778, ending up questioning whether Litzia's husband, Charles Buonaparte fathered them all. Napoleon was not baptized until two years

Napoleon Bonaparte, 1792, as Lieutenant Colonel of the 1st Battalion of Corsica, painted by Henri Felix Phillipoteaux in 1834. Musée National du Chateau de Versailles et de Trianon

after his birth when a double baptism was held along with his newly born sister, Maria-Anna, in the Cathedral of Ajaccio on 21 July 1771.

Despite local records that seemingly attest to Charles Buonaparte's primary schooling in Corte and university in Pisa, according to the late James Alexander Stuart, royal genealogical Stuart papers handed down and now in his possession, allege that Napoleon's real name was not Buonaparte, but rather Napoleon 'de Boveria de Rohano Stuardo' – in other words a lineal descendant of King Charles II by his first illegitimate child, James de Rohano Stuardo (Principe de Boveria) born in 1647. Certainly correspondence concerning the latter, surviving at the Jesuit Curia in Rome, contains not only Stuart royal seals but also confirmation by Queen Christina of Sweden of this royal birth to Charles II, written as she travelled through Hamburg on

Napoleon's Barge with Crown, signalling 'royal' lineage. Musée de la Marine, Palais de Chaillot, Paris. Photograph by David Baldwin

her way to Rome.[2] On this basis, Cardinal Fesch would have been his half-uncle while Napoleon's grandmother would have been Marie de Neuhoff, titular Queen of Corsica (daughter of King Theodore of Corsica). His father, Charles Marie, was allegedly born at Kinvalla, Brittany, in 1746, only in his teens returning to family estates in Corsica to assume the name 'Buonaparte'.[3] Even the birth date of his mother, Letizia, is uncertain because of the destruction by fire of the Ajaccio archives in 1789.

The late Michael, styled Count of Albany, claiming to be a royal Stuart descendant, retained in his archive a family tree[4] which traces Napoleon's forbears as follows:

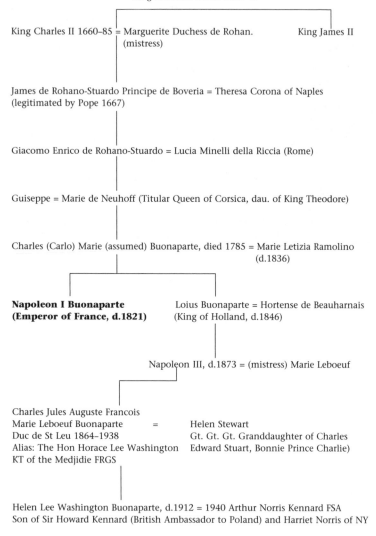

King Charles I Stuart 1625–49

King Charles II 1660–85 = Marguerite Duchess de Rohan.   King James II
                            (mistress)

James de Rohano-Stuardo Principe de Boveria = Theresa Corona of Naples
(legitimated by Pope 1667)

Giacomo Enrico de Rohano-Stuardo = Lucia Minelli della Riccia (Rome)

Guiseppe = Marie de Neuhoff (Titular Queen of Corsica, dau. of King Theodore)

Charles (Carlo) Marie (assumed) Buonaparte, died 1785 = Marie Letizia Ramolino
                                                            (d.1836)

Napoleon I Buonaparte   Loius Buonaparte = Hortense de Beauharnais
(Emperor of France, d.1821)   (King of Holland, d.1846)

Napoleon III, d.1873 = (mistress) Marie Leboeuf

Charles Jules Auguste Francois
Marie Leboeuf Buonaparte   =   Helen Stewart
Duc de St Leu 1864–1938   Gt. Gt. Gt. Granddaughter of Charles
Alias: The Hon Horace Lee Washington   Edward Stuart, Bonnie Prince Charlie)
KT of the Medjidie FRGS

Helen Lee Washington Buonaparte, d.1912 = 1940 Arthur Norris Kennard FSA
Son of Sir Howard Kennard (British Ambassador to Poland) and Harriet Norris of NY

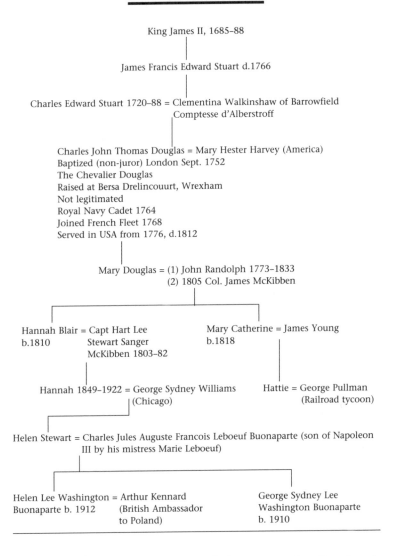

King James II, 1685–88

James Francis Edward Stuart d.1766

Charles Edward Stuart 1720–88 = Clementina Walkinshaw of Barrowfield
Comptesse d'Alberstroff

Charles John Thomas Douglas = Mary Hester Harvey (America)
Baptized (non-juror) London Sept. 1752
The Chevalier Douglas
Raised at Bersa Drelincouurt, Wrexham
Not legitimated
Royal Navy Cadet 1764
Joined French Fleet 1768
Served in USA from 1776, d.1812

Mary Douglas = (1) John Randolph 1773–1833
(2) 1805 Col. James McKibben

Hannah Blair = Capt Hart Lee
b.1810   Stewart Sanger
             McKibben 1803–82

Mary Catherine = James Young
b.1818

Hannah 1849–1922 = George Sydney Williams
(Chicago)

Hattie = George Pullman
(Railroad tycoon)

Helen Stewart = Charles Jules Auguste Francois Leboeuf Buonaparte (son of Napoleon
III by his mistress Marie Leboeuf)

Helen Lee Washington = Arthur Kennard
Buonaparte b. 1912   (British Ambassador
                         to Poland)

George Sydney Lee
Washington Buonaparte
b. 1910

If correct,[5] it appears such speculation concerning Napoleon's royal Stuart parentage was kept from Queen Victoria upon her State Visit to France in 1855, by which time she found herself standing at the Hotel des Invalides on the South Bank of the River Seine in Paris: 'There I stood at the arm of Napoleon III, his nephew, before the coffin of England's greatest foe: I, the great grand-daughter of that King who hated him most, and who most vigorously opposed him, and this very nephew, who bears his name, being my nearest and dearest ally!'⁶ Quite to what extent the Emperor Napoleon I had taken his nominal Roman Catholic allegiance seriously in his personal life remains somewhat of a mystery. In public he was certainly not in fear of challenging papal authority in secular matters of empire, being himself crowned King of Italy in 1805, and is on record as having responded to the heavy French losses in battle with the comment: 'A single night in the brothels of Paris will replace that lot'. In fact he was to oversee 1.4 million French casualties throughout a span of 17 years.

But Queen Victoria's State Visit to his nephew was a reciprocal gesture in return for Napoleon III's imperial visit to Windsor and London earlier in the year between 16 and 21 April, during which Prince Albert was to comment dryly: 'I shall have to have precautions taken in the Crypt of St George's Chapel to see that George III does not turn in his grave.'⁷ The visit to Britain had been wisely crafted with Napoleon III's Catholicism in mind to last from a Monday to a Saturday so as to save the Emperor, his wife and retinue from having to spend a Sunday in England. Upon the return visit to France, Queen Victoria and Prince Albert, together with their retinue, boarded the Royal Yacht *Victoria and Albert*, sailing for Boulogne. This visit was to span two Sundays, with the British Court attending services in their own private apartments, Lord Cowley issuing a hint that what The Queen would most appreciate would be brevity in the sermon. Napoleon III had visited the Crystal Palace at Sydenham and surveyed the wonders of the British Empire contained therein, and now in Paris Queen Victoria was to visit the Exposition Universalle in return. However, it was the visit to Les Invalides that captured the visit.

From Queen Marie-Antoinette's former apartments in the royal palace where they were thoughtfully housed by Napoleon III, the royal party ventured to view the remains of Napoleon as a consequence of the decision taken by King Louis Phillippe in 1840, when he had decided to attract more support for his fading regime by appealing to the name of Napoleon. With this in mind he had Emperor Napoleon's statue hoisted atop the Vendome column and the Arc de Triomphe completed. He then arranged, with Lord Palmerston's agreement, to have Naploleon's body repatriated from the island of Saint Helena. On 16 December 1840 the Emperor Napoleon's coffin was hauled by 16 horses through the streets of Paris for a funeral service and laid to rest on a huge catafalque under the dome of Les Invalides. This had necessitated the removal of the altar with Thackeray concluding 'And why not? Who is God here but Napoleon?'[8] It turned out to be a move that deposed Louis Phillippe from the throne, for in 1848 the French people voted for the return of another Bonaparte – now hosting the royal party. Queen Victoria had struggled to reconcile herself to this turn of events, but standing in Les Invalides the Napoleonic legend pervaded the atmosphere to take on a whole life of its own – and was to lead to the most extraordinary royal prayer for ensuing peace.

Napoleon's coffin had been removed from the catafalque and lay in a side chapel while a special central crypt was being constructed for his remains. This had not been completed, so Queen Victoria continued past its balustrade to the side chapel where she observed the coffin covered with a violet pall, glittering all over with the golden bees of Clovis – as it happens the founder of the royal lines of Stuart and France – the hat Napoleon had worn at Eylau, the sword he used at Austerlitz and the plaque of the Legion d'Honneur. Around the chapel stood veterans of the First Empire carrying torches. The royal party, comprising by now Queen Victoria, Prince Albert, the Prince of Wales and the Princess Royal, Emperor Napoleon III and Princess Mathilde, stood for several minutes in silence, broken by rumbles of thunder. Then Queen Victoria turned to the Prince of Wales, put her hand on his shoulder, and said 'Kneel down before the tomb of the Great Napoleon'.[9] Bertie knelt as directed but at that moment nothing more could be said for there was an almighty crash of thunder, which echoed around the vaults, with lightning whitening the torches, accompanied throughout by hissing from a deluge of rain pouring down. At that moment an organist struck up the National Anthem. The moment passed, the Prince of Wales got to his feet, and the party returned through the driving rain to their carriages: 'Strange and wonderful indeed!' commented Queen Victoria, who went on to record in her diary: 'It seems as if in this tribute of respect to a departed and great foe, old enmities and rivalries were wiped out, and the seal of heaven placed upon that bond of amity which is now happily established between two great nations! May heaven bless and prosper it!'[10]

It was not to be, for many British people retained distrust of Napoleon III's intentions, and detected a dormant desire to avenge his uncle's defeat at Waterloo in 1815. This is tinged with irony when it turns out that Napoleon and Wellington were brothers in law. This comes about through the marriage of Jérôme Bonaparte, Napoleon's youngest brother. Jérôme had been a lieutenant in the French Navy in 1803, deployed to the Caribbean, where, to avoid capture by the British, he was forced to land and take refuge in the United States of America. He journeyed to New York, and then went on to Baltimore to rendezvous with an American whom he had befriended in the French Navy. There he met, and married within two months, Elizabeth Patterson, daughter of William, an Irish immigrant gunrunner during the Revolution. They were married by the Archbishop of Baltimore on Christmas Eve 1803, in the cathedral.

Although not yet Emperor, Jérôme's brother Napoleon reacted with fury, had the marriage annulled by the French courts and ordered his brother back without 'the young person'. Jérôme went back but accompanied by 'Betsy'. She was denied entry to France and went instead to London, where she gave birth to a son in 1805. Jérôme, meanwhile, did the bidding of his brother and returned to duty with the French Navy. He subsequently married Frederica Catherine, daughter of the King of Württemberg, in 1807, and became King of Westphalia. Betsy on the other hand returned to Baltimore with her son who, in turn, had two sons. One became a colonel in his cousin Napoleon III's army; the other became Attorney-General of the United States of America from 1906 to 1909, dying in 1921. The colonel's only son died in 1945, thus ending the line. But Betsy's (i.e. Elizabeth Patterson's) brother's widow remarried to the 1st Marquess Wellesley as his second wife. Being the elder brother of Arthur Duke of Wellington, this act made Napoleon and Wellington brothers-in-law!

Napoleon's elder brother, Joseph Bonaparte, also settled in the United States of America, in different circumstances, but with many treasures acquired from Europe. He had first been placed on a diplomatic mission under the Consulate in 1800 to reconcile differences between France and the United States of America, before becoming King of Naples until 1808, and then King of Spain until he abdicated in 1813 under pressure from Wellington's victories in the Peninsular War, finally fleeing to the United States of America upon Napoleon's defeat at Waterloo. Accompanied by his daughter Zenaide and her husband Prince Charles, another daughter Charlotte, and his secretary Louis Maillard, Joseph Bonaparte took the title Comte de Survilliers, and acquired Point Breeze in 1816 as part of a 1,000-acre country estate. There he created a lake from Crosswicke Creek, about 200 yards wide and half a mile long, with islands and a bridge, and built two houses for the others and a mansion for himself, incorporating a most curious feature. The mansion was connected to the creek's bank by a long underground tunnel. Although the original mansion was burned in 1820, the mysterious tunnel to the river survives, although now broken through in several places. Joseph Bonaparte built a new mansion on the site of the former stable east of the lake, which he occupied until 1839. He then retired to Europe, dying in Florence in 1844. His grandson Joseph disposed of the Point Breeze estate and its contents in 1847, with furnishings and a magnificent art collection, including works by Rubens, Snyders and Rembrandt, being sold at auction. It is conjectured that the tunnel was used to store all manner of valuable works 'looted' from Europe.

Returning to Napoleon III, his invasion of Italy shocked Queen Victoria as his true intentions and ambitions surfaced. The Franco-Prussian War brought about rapid developments, however, and in six weeks the downfall of Napoleon III with surrender at the Battle of Sedan. Empress Eugenie fled to England where she was re-enfolded in Queen Victoria's family circle and treated with much affection amid mounting tragedy. Napoleon III himself died on the eve of his ambitious planned 'Return from Elba' and a few years later their only child, the Prince

Imperial, was killed fighting in the British Army in the Zulu War. This was to lead to another royal prayer of great poignancy.

The Prince Imperial had ridden out with a small scouting party on 1 June 1879, only to be surprised, while bivouacking, by a band of Zulus. All escaped but Louis, whose horse bolted, and he was left entirely alone to face the advancing Zulus, who testified that he fought 'like a lion', dying of 17 wounds – all in front. Not until the following morning did a well-armed search party set out to recover his body. It was taken to Cape Town and placed aboard HMS *Orontes*. The shock was unimaginable for Empress Eugenie. But despite the temptation to apportion blame as further details emerged and a captain was singled out for court-martial proceedings for cowardice (perhaps as a scapegoat for higher command failings already associated with the Isandhlwana fiasco), the Empress intervened before the Duke of Cambridge gave the final verdict, with a plea and prayer:

> the one earthy consolation I have is the idea that my beloved child fell as a soldier, obeying orders, on a duty which was commanded, and that those who gave them did so because they thought him competent and useful. Enough of recriminations. Let the memory of his death unite in a common sorrow all those who loved him, and let no-one suffer, either in his reputation or his interests. I who desire nothing more on earth, ask it as a last prayer.[11]

The upshot was the acquittal of the captain as the sentence was read in the Natal Court Martial, though he died an unhappy, shunned, man in India four years later. The matter of Louis' funeral remained, and Queen Victoria determined to give him magnificent funeral honours for his burial at St Mary's, Chislehurst, beside his father, Napoleon III. A number of princes, headed by the Prince of Wales met the body off HMS *Orontes* at Woolwich on 11 July, and the next day, after resting overnight at the family home in Chislehurst (Camden Place), the Prince of Wales, the Duke of Edinburgh, the Duke of Connaught and the Prince Royal of Sweden attended the funeral, acting as pall-bearers to the gun carriage, which itself was draped in a Union Flag and Tricoleur, accompanied by 200 army cadets, the band of the Royal Artillery and the Bishop of Constantine. Queen Victoria ventured, 'This was the end of all that was once so splendid and brilliant, and of one who promised to be a blessing not only to his country, but to the world'.

Yet Queen Victoria went further in an attempt to assuage Eugenie's inconsolable grief. She gave orders for a cross to be erected on the site of the hollow in which the Prince Imperial met his death. The 'Queen's Cross Expedition' lugged the simple stone cross from Pietermaritzburg to Zululand, where it stood ready for Eugenie's pilgrimage bearing the inscription:

> This cross is erected by Queen Victoria in affectionate remembrance of Napoleon Eugene Louis Jean Joseph Prince Imperial to mark the spot where while assisting in a reconnaissance with British troops on 1st June 1879 he was attacked by a party of Zulus and fell with his face to the foe.

Eugenie spent the night of the first anniversary of Louis' death in prayer beside the Queen's cross, recording:

> More than once I noticed black forms on the top of the banks, which moved silently about and watched me through the tall grasses. This scrutiny was full of curiosity, but it was not hostile. I believe these savages wished rather to express their sympathy and their pity ... and doubtless they were the very men who had killed my son on the same spot. Towards morning a strange thing happened. Although there was not a breath of air, the flames of the candles were suddenly deflected, as if someone wished to extinguish them, and I said to him: 'Is it indeed you beside me? Do you wish me to go away?'[12]

At that she rose and retreated to her tent. An attempt to have a memorial placed in Westminster Abbey fell foul of a parliamentary vote and divided public feeling, so Queen Victoria had it installed at St George's Chapel, Windsor, instead.

In 1979 The Queen paid the first official visit by a reigning monarch to the Roman Catholic Westminster Cathedral – in this case for their flower festival. This turned out to be almost 100 years to the day after Queen Victoria had laid her wreath at the Roman Catholic Church of St Mary's, Chislehurst Common, for the French Prince Imperial's funeral there. Queen Victoria waited and then went to the Church five days after the funeral to lay her wreath. It was not until 8 February 1908 that a reigning monarch was again to visit a Roman Catholic church officially. The occasion for this was the Requiem Mass for the murdered King Carlos and Crown Prince of Portugal at St James's, Spanish Place, near Manchester Square in Marylebone. King Edward VII, Queen Alexandra and the Prince and Princess of Wales all attended.

Notes

[1] Recollections of Gaspard Monge published in P. Bartel, *La Jeunesse inédite de Napoléon: d'aprés de nombreux documents* (Paris: Amiot-Dumont, Presses des Imprimeries Réunies de Chambéry, 1954). Copies at the National Art Library of the Victoria and Albert Mueseum, and Wellington Museum, Apsley House: catalogue number: WEL5.J.12

[2] Archivum Romanum Societas Jesu, Borgo S Spirito, Rome: Opp.NN 174/175:E. In this folder is to be found Queen Christina's letter of attestation of James de la Cloche's (Stuart) royal birth, including the description therein where she writes of him as 'filius naturalis Caroles: Regis angliae ...' and signs there 'Christina Alexandra'. This letter, in Christina's own hand, is sealed with her own signet ring covering the bottom arms of the letter 'A', indicating it was applied afterwards in the conventional manner. The collection also contains a large number of other letters written in 1668 between Charles II and Oliva, the Jesuit General in Rome, concerning payments for the welfare and whereabouts of James de la Cloche, nearly all those purporting to be from Charles II also sealed with his royal seals. Arguments about the possibility of the collection being a forgery are discounted by the incontestably genuine attestation from Queen Christina, whose letter upon this matter matches not only the peculiarity of her handwriting in her extant correspondence from Uppsala with Karl Gustav, but also in the use of particular water-marked paper. For further details of the handwriting, water marks, sigillography and provenance of this collection see D. Baldwin, 'The Politico-Religious Usage of The Queen's Chapel, 1623–1688', M.Litt., Durham University, 1999, pp. 107–13, 187, 188, 199, 200. One letter (Opp NN 174/175, DII,5) describes the arrangements outlined by King Charles II in 1668 to the Jesuit General, Oliva, for James de la Cloche to visit his father in England. Upon arrival in London he

should 'present himself to the Queen Consort, rather when at Mass in our palace of St James, or when she goes to visit our dear and most honoured mother, to whom he will present a letter, sealed as a petition, in which he will briefly state who he is: and her Majesty has received Our orders to do what is necessary to introduce him to Us with all possible care' (in the 'Litterae Caroli II Regis Angliae de filio suo naturali Iacobo de la Cloche, qui Domum Probationis').

³ Micheal of Albany, *The Forgotten Monarchy of Scotland* (Shaftesbury: Element, 1998), p. 233.

⁴ Micheal of Albany, *The Forgotten Monarchy of Scotland* (Shaftesbury: Element, 1998), Chart D, p. 476.

⁵ The ancestors of Napoleon delineated by Michael of Albany's do not accord with Napoleon Bonaparte's family tree as detailed in the Napoleonic Museum in Rome's copy of Cutonei, Niccolo Jeno 'La famiglia Bonaparte dal 1185 fino al 1854', Inventory Number MN 10690, or that in the *Official Guide to Visiting The Napoleonic Museum* (Rome, Gangemi Editore, 1997). Neither of these, though, cite entirely convincing primary sources with regard to Napoleon's parentage.

⁶ *Leaves from a Journal: A Record of the Visit of the Emperor and Empress of the French and of the Visit of the Queen and HRH the Prince Consort to the Emperor of the French, 1855,* edited by R. Mortimer (New York: Farrar, Straus and Cudahy, 1961).

⁷ *Leaves from a Journal: A Record of the Visit of the Emperor and Empress of the French and of the Visit of the Queen and HRH the Prince Consort to the Emperor of the French, 1855,* edited by R. Mortimer (New York: Farrar, Straus and Cudahy, 1961)..

⁸ W.M. Thackeray, *The Second Funeral of Napoleon* (New York: John W Lovell, 1883).

⁹ *Leaves from a Journal: A Record of the Visit of the Emperor and Empress of the French and of the Visit of the Queen and HRH the Prince Consort to the Emperor of the French, 1855,* edited by R. Mortimer (New York: Farrar, Straus and Cudahy, 1961).

¹⁰ *Leaves from a Journal: A Record of the Visit of the Emperor and Empress of the French and of the Visit of the Queen and HRH the Prince Consort to the Emperor of the French, 1855,* edited by R. Mortimer (New York: Farrar, Straus and Cudahy, 1961).

¹¹ Des Garets, Marie Comtesse de Larminat de Garnier, *Souvenirs d'une Demoiselle d'Honneur: Impératrice Eugénie en exile* (Paris: Calmann-Levy, 1928).

¹² A. Filon, *Souvenirs sur l'Impératrice Eugenie* (Paris: Calmann-Levy, 1920).

6

'Royal' Prayers of America

since preservation of the sacred fire of liberty and the destiny of
the republican model of government are justly considered as
deeply, perhaps finally, staked of the experiment . . . I shall take
my present leave; but not without resorting once more to the
Benign Parent of the Human Race. (George Washington, 1789)

There exists an extraordinary assertion[1] that in his successful
military prosecution of the Colonial War from 1776 to 1781,
more commonly called the American War of Independence,

*George Washington as Colonel of the Virginia Regiment, 1772, painted by George
Wilson Peale, Washington-Custis-Lee Collection, Washington and Lee University,
Lexington, Virginia*

George Washington had not intended to create a republic. His true intentions, according to the assertion, were revealed upon General Charles Cornwallis's surrender of British forces at Yorktown, Virginia, in October 1781.

Before glancing at the assertion, it must be noted that no corroborative evidence has yet been found of the 'text' upon which it largely relies. Moreover, at least two of the alleged chief participants in 1782 cited as originator and curator of it, namely, 'The Hon Charles Hervey-Townsend (later Britain's Ambassador to the Hague)' and his aunt 'Lady Molly Carteron, Countess of Manorwater', remain unidentifiable either by name or occupation – unless there has been careless transcription of their names.

Historians have dismissed the whole alleged corpus as bogus and a forgery, not least because while there was, indeed, an Extraordinary Ambassador to The Hague by the name of Townshend, he was Charles, 2nd Viscount Townsend, who served as Ambassador to the Congress at the Hague from 1709 to 1724 and who died in 1738. The author of the assertion also claimed that a copy of the text written by the Hon. Charles Hervey-Townsend 'is well documented in the USA Senate Archives, and in the Manorwater Papers'.[2]

However, in 1999 papers of a junior branch of the Townshend family of Raynham in Norfolk came to light in an auction.[3] This collection had originally been housed at Frognal, Chislehurst, in Kent. Among this corpus were found the papers of 'John Thomas Townshend, 2nd Viscount Sydney, including letters to his father (series including letter written at The Hague and Berlin, 1780s, 1790s)',[4] together with letters to his wife and 'aunt Mary', and an autograph account of his travels in the Netherlands (unsigned) comprising 20 papers in 1786.

It is quite possible, therefore, that there has been careless scholarship in recording the provenance of the documentary evidence asserted in support of the author's original assertions, and that the 'Townsend' to whom reference is made was John Thomas Townhsend, 2nd Viscount Sydney. John was son of the Hon. Thomas Townshend, 1st Viscount Sydney (the man who gave his name to 'Sydney Cove' in Australia, the latter choosing

*'Frognal House', seat of the Townshend family, by George Shepherd as it appears in
W.H. Ireland's* New and Complete History of the County of Kent *(London:
George Virtue, 1828). The image is after the formal gardens were replaced with a
'Capability Brown' landscape*

his title deliberately to indicate his family origin from Saint
Denis in France) rather than the illusive 'Hervey Townsend'.

It is known from the Townshend papers that emerged from
Frognal, and were sold in 1999, that John Thomas Townshend
was not only at The Hague in the 1780s and 1790s, and writing
from there in various directions, but also visited Berlin, and
travelled extensively in Europe at the very time it is alleged a
Townshend who had later connections with The Hague
witnessed a constitutional meeting with Bonnie Prince Charlie
in Florence in 1782. Furthermore, the Frognal Archive reveals
that John Townshend had an aunt, Mary, to whom he wrote,
and these letters have survived. On the basis of continued poor
transcription from an original text, 'Lady Molly Carteron' may
have been 'Mary'.

Although much more research is now needed in this area, the
recent emergence of these papers reopens the possibility that
there may, after all, be substance to the assertion

The author of the assertion, published by 'Michael of Albany'
in 1998,[5] avers the following to have happened. It was just 35

years since Bonnie Prince Charlie's defeat at the Battle of Culloden in 1746, and he was now resident in exile at the Palazzo San Clemente in the Via San Sebastiano, Florence. In November 1782 a legal mission from George Washington arrived, comprising Mr Galloway of Maryland, two brothers with the name Sylvester, and Mr Fish, a lawyer from New York, carrying official Letters of Credence. These were presented to the exiled Stuart 'King' in his salon, and witnessed there by 'The Hon. Charles Harvey-Townshend, Britain's later Ambassador to The Hague',[6] in company with two cousins of Bonnie Prince Charlie. One of these was Guiseppe de Rohano Stuardo (grandson of James de Rohano Stuardo, illegitimate son of King Charles II and, the author also alleges, Napoleon Bonarparte's paternal grandfather) and 'Comtesse Marguerite de Massillan' (a 'cousin by descent from Charles II'[7] who was to marry Bonnie Prince Charlie on 26 December 1785 at the Church of the Holy Apostles, Rome, opposite the Palazzo Muti). In 1782, therefore, Bonnie Prince Charlie was separated from his first wife, Louise of Stolberg, and it was by no means certain that he would remarry and father a male heir.

What happened next was allegedly recorded personally by Harvey-Townshend who sent a written transcript of the proceedings to 'his aunt Lady Mplly Carteron, Countess of Manorwater'.[8] With military victory secured, Washington's emissaries were able to proceed more confidently than the men of Boston who had first approached the Stuart 'King' in Holland back at the beginning of the Colonial War.

By now urgent debate was joined about what form of governance should be adopted in consequence of the 'Declaration by the Representatives of the United States of America in General Congress Assembled' made in Philadelphia on 4 July 1776, when Blackstone's 1774 *Commentaries on the Laws of England* was the standard textbook used by the delegates, containing as it did the passage: 'There is and must be in every state a supreme, irresistible, absolute and uncontrolled authority, in which the ... rights of sovereignty reside. This supreme power is by the constitution of Great Britain vested in the King, Lords and Commons'. This was anathema to many famous free-thinking philosophers such as Thomas Paine who wished to influence the future governmental system of the fledgling United States and have been fêted for their achievement. Yet the adoption of republicanism was by no means the inevitable outcome of these debates.

Now in Florence in 1782, following some general discussion and introductions, Mr Galloway of Maryland allegedly addressed the exiled Stuart 'King' thus:

> Sir, we have letters, one especially which gives us the authority to offer the Crown of America to the rightful King of Great Britain. I have told you that we in America are not yet wholly republicans, although there are those among our people who favour a republic. But they are still a minority. We may have got rid of a king who misgoverned us, but we have no wish to get rid of kingship. We want a king of our own choosing, and would get with him all the ancient sanctions of monarchy ... [9]

Bonnie Prince Charlie had previously commented of their trip to Europe: 'you take an excellent way of meditation in visiting this museum. Here you see the relics of any government you please – a dozen republics, tyrannies, theocracies, merchant confederations, kingdoms, and more than one empire. You have your choice'.[10]

Mr Fish reaffirmed their intention and the origin of their mission:

> Sir, we have the opportunity to start afresh, with a clean page to write upon. We believe that the way abides peacefully in a royal house, with ciphers who dignify without obstructing a popular constitution. We come to you with the reasoned conclusion of the men who achieved liberty. General Washington shares our views, and has asked Mr Hamilton to send us on this mission.[11]

The upshot was eventual refusal by Bonnie Prince Charlie on the basis that his own succession was in doubt and therefore America's governance too if he were to accept. In refusing, though, he let loose an astonishing fact: 'I have travelled far; I was even begged to join your Party in '75, but even then I refused, with hope to regain Scotland and England', indicating the approach made in Holland to him in 1775 by the men of Boston. He closed by saying:

Nay, Sir, you and your friends tell Mr Hamilton and General Washington that I was flattered by the thought, but I am too old. I have failed most of my life, and have no wish to fail more. Thank you Gentlemen, but this is my answer – my last word on the subject. Let us think no more upon it.[12]

Should any corroborative primary documentary evidence turn up to substantiate the assertions of 'Michael of Albany' one could then conclude, in the light of the mission to Bonnie Prince Charlie, that any prayers of George Washington identified as earlier than 1782 were of a monarchical persuasion, and still of royal approbation as a system of acceptable government.

Although a case be advanced for John Thomas Townsend, a yet more likely 'Townsend' candidate for being the personage visiting Prince Charlie in 1782 was his father, the Hon. Thomas Townsend, 2nd Viscount Sidney. Born in 1733 and dying in 1800, Thomas Townsend served as Secretary at War from March until July 1782 under the second Rockingham ministry, and then upon Lord Shelburne becoming Prime Minister in July 1782 succeeded him as Home Secretary, resigning in April 1783, only to be reappointed on 23 December 1783. He was awarded with the Baronetcy of Chislehurst in 1783 specifically for his services in bringing hostilities to an end with the United States of America through advocating close commercial ties with the new American state while also arguing that Britain had a moral duty to compensate loyalists for their losses. The implication that Thomas Townsend was deeply involved secretly in the American colonial settlement cannot readily be dismissed. Britain, through canny recognition of American independence, and against all the prevailing military odds, managed to squeeze out the powerful French presence in North America by means of a surprise peace treaty on 30 November 1782 between the United States of America and Britain, in advance of the later Treaty of Paris in 1783.[13] The timing of the November 1782 treaty, so enthusiastically embraced by Benjamin Franklin, appears neatly to coincide with the failure of Washington's 'Fish Mission' earlier that month in Florence. All, then, was set fair by a pioneering treaty that was to bring about the transatlantic 'special relationship' between Britain and the United States of America.

Moving on from assertion to incontestable fact, in resigning his commission as General of the Continental Army on 23 December 1783, George Washington said: 'I consider it an indispensable duty to close this last solemn act of my official life by commending the interests of our dearest country to the protection of Almighty God and those who have the superintendence of them into His holy keeping.' If Michael of Albany's assertion is correct, by then Washington would have received his emissaries' reply from Florence and resigned himself to a forthcoming republican system of government, and was therefore seeking the Almighty's blessing upon it. But even by 25 September 1789, when asked to designate a day of prayer and thanksgiving following the previous day's resolution of the House of Representatives, he studiously avoided mention of systems of government and chose instead to declare the act of 'Thanksgiving' as a public holiday in the words:

> It is the duty of all nations to acknowledge the providence of Almighty God, to obey His will, to be grateful for His mercy, to implore His protection and favour ... That the great and glorious Being who is the beneficent author of all the good that was, that is, or that ever will be, that we may then unite in rendering unto Him our sincere and humble thanks for His care and protection of the people ...[14]

But what are we therefore to make of George Washington's prayers before any alleged constitutional watershed of 1782? His apocryphal prayer at Valley Forge as the Continental Army hunkered down, demoralized after the British Redcoat victories at Brandywine and Germantown, just north of Philadelphia, in 1777 has been dismissed in some quarters as simply untrue.[15] Yet if there is some element of authentic recollection by Pastor Potts who claimed to be an eyewitness of General Washington's prayer, it is certainly not out of character with these attestable later utterances. He is credited by the Revd Nathaniel Randolph Snowden, a Presbyterian minister and graduate of Princeton born in 1770, in his *Diary of Remembrance* (the original of which is owned by the Historical Society of Pennsylvania): 'I knew personally the celebrated Quaker Potts who saw Gen'l Washington alone in the woods at prayer. I got it from himself'. Snowden was riding with Potts in Montgomery County, Pennsylvania, near Valley Forge, when Potts recalled:

There laid the army of Washington. It was a most distressing time of ye war, and all were for giving up the Ship but that great and good man. In that woods (pointing to a close in view) I heard a plaintive sound as, of a man at prayer. I tied my horse to a sapling & went quietly into the woods & to my astonishment I saw the great George Washington on his knees alone, with his sword on one side and his cocked hat on the other. He was at Prayer to the God of the Armies, beseeching to interpose with his Divine aid, as it was ye Crisis, & the cause of the country, of humanity & of the world. Such a prayer I never heard from the lips of man. I left him alone praying'.

Other versions credit the Marquis de Lafayette and General Muhlenberg as the witnesses.

George Washington's inaugural address to Congress upon taking oath on 30 April 1789 as President contained a fascinating hesitation about whether

in the important revolution just accomplished in the system of their United government, the tranquil deliberations and voluntary consent of so many distinct communities, from which the event has resulted can not be compared with the means by which most governments have been established without some return of pious gratitude along with an humble anticipation of the future blessings which the past seem to presage.[16]

The implication was that if the experiment proved unsuccessful over time, then a return to traditional monarchical government might be in store:

We ought to be no less persuaded that the propitious smiles of Heaven can never be expected on a nation that disregards the eternal rules of order and right which Heaven itself has ordained; and since preservation of the sacred fire of liberty and the destiny of the republican model of government are justly considered as deeply, perhaps finally, staked on the experiment entrusted to the hands of the American people ... I shall take my present leave; but not without resorting once more to the Benign Parent of the Human Race, in humble supplication that, since He has been pleased to favour the American people with opportunities for deliberating in perfect tranquillity, and dispositions for deciding with unparalleled unanimity on a form of government for the security of their union and the advancement of their happiness, so His divine blessings may be equally conspicuous in the enlarged views, the temperate consultations and the wise measures on which the success of this Government must depend.

Notes

[1] Prince Michael of Albany, *The Forgotten Monarchy of Scotland* (Shaftesbury: Element, 1998).

[2] Prince Michael of Albany, *The Forgotten Monarchy of Scotland* (Shaftesbury: Element, 1998), p. 214.

[3] Lot 188 in Artfact Auction House, UK, 1999, and description of contents placed at www.artfact.com/auction-lot/archive-of-the-townshend-family.

[4] Quoted from 1999 Artfact Auction House description of Lot 188 at www.artfact.com/auction-lot/archive-of-the-townshend-family.

[5] Prince Michael of Albany, *The Forgotten Monarchy of Scotland* (Shaftesbury: Element, 1998).

[6] Prince Michael of Albany, *The Forgotten Monarchy of Scotland* (Shaftesbury: Element, 1998), pp. 213–14.

[7] Prince Michael, of Albany *The Forgotten Monarchy of Scotland* (Shaftesbury: Element, 1998), pp 214–17.

[8] Prince Michael of Albany, *The Forgotten Monarchy of Scotland* (Shaftesbury: Element, 1998), p. 214.

[9] Transcript published as Appendix VII in Albany, Prince Michael of Albany, *The Forgotten Monarchy of Scotland* (Shaftesbury: Element, 1998), pp. 365–7, purportedly representing text of a letter from the Hon. Hervey-Townsend to Lady Molly Carteron, Countess of Manor-water, in 'private papers of the Manorwater family', recording conversation with the United States representatives at the Palazzo San Clemente, Via San Sebastiano, Florence, in November 1782.

[10] Transcript published as Appendix VII in Albany, Prince Michael of

Albany, *The Forgotten Monarchy of Scotland* (Shaftesbury: Element, 1998), pp. 365-7, purportedly representing text of a letter from the Hon. Hervey-Townsend to Lady Molly Carteron, Countess of Manorwater, in 'private papers of the Manorwater family', recording conversation with the United States representatives at the Palazzo San Clemente, Via San Sebastiano, Florence, in November 1782.

11 Transcript published as Appendix VII in Albany, Prince Michael of Albany, *The Forgotten Monarchy of Scotland* (Shaftesbury: Element, 1998), pp. 365-7 purportedly representing text of a letter from the Hon. Hervey-Townsend to Lady Molly Carteron, Countess of Manorwater, in 'private papers of the Manorwater family', recording conversation with the United States representatives at the Palazzo San Clemente, Via San Sebastiano, Florence, in November 1782.

12 Transcript published as Appendix VII in Albany, Prince Michael of Albany, *The Forgotten Monarchy of Scotland* (Shaftesbury: Element, 1998), pp. 365-7 purportedly representing text of a letter from the Hon. Hervey-Townsend to Lady Molly Carteron, Countess of Manorwater, in 'private papers of the Manorwater family', recording conversation with the United States representatives at the Palazzo San Clemente, Via San Sebastiano, Florence, in November 1782.

13 At the celebrations in Passy, the strategic victory of the emerging Anglo-American peace in November 1782 was soon became evident in a conversation between British delegate, Caleb Whitefoord, and a French guest, the former responding to the latter's observation that 'the thirteen United States would form the greatest empire in all the world' with the comment 'Yes, Monsieur, ... and they will all speak English, every one of 'em'; W.A. Shewins (ed.), *Whitefoord Papers* (Oxford: Oxford University Press, 1898), vol. i, p. 87.

14 J.D. Richardson (ed.), *Compilation of the Messages and Papers of the Presidents, 1789-1797*, 10 vols (New York, 1969), vol. I, p. 64.

15 'Parson Weems and Bishop William Meade, tried to make out Washington as more religious than he was – Weems relates that he was found praying in a wood near Valley Forge, by Quaker Poots, and Meade has him strongly opposed to swearing, drinking, dancing, theatre-going, and hunting – all untrue' in P. Johnson, *A History of the American People* (London: Weidenfeld and Nicolson, 1997), p. 171.

16 *Washington's Inaugural Address of 30th April 1789*, Records of the U.S. Senate, Record Group 46, National Archives. Original Washington signature is found on this document.

7

A Prophecy of 1732 Written in the Year of George Washington's Birth

George Washington's own religious tenets and political objectives have come under scrutiny of late, with a number of largely unsubstantiated extrapolations made from the fact that he had been initiated on 4 November 1752 into the Fredericksburg Lodge Number 4, Virginia, as a Rosicrucian Mason, passing on 3 March 1753 and raised on 4 August 1753. He became a Templar Mason by 1768 and was elected Grand Master of the Templar Alexandria, Lodge Number 22 in Virginia, on 28 April 1788. He used the Holy Bible of St John's Lodge Number 1 of New York City when taking the Oath of Office as President of the United States of America; the Oath being administered by Grand Master Robert Livingstone, Chancellor of New York.

From the undisputed fact that many of Washington's co-founders of the United States of America turn out to have been Freemasons, all kinds of speculative theories have been advanced. He has been cited as appointing Pierre Charles L'Enfant, an engineer in the continental army, in 1791 as the architect of the proposed new capital city, on ground selected by Washington that he termed the 'Territory of Columbia' for building 'Washingtonople'. L'Enfant's original plan has been interpreted by some as incorporating Masonic symbols, and although Washington dismissed him in 1792, the eventual execution of the city plan has been interpreted as nevertheless maintaining significant Masonic symbolism.

The theory advanced is that if the Capitol building forms the top of a compass, the left leg of the compass becomes Pennsylvania Avenue, standing now on the Jefferson Memorial, while the right leg is Maryland Avenue. The square is formed by Canal Street and Louisiana Avenue. Inverted pentagrams and other symbolism are also allegedly identified. The whole alignment of the city has also been alleged by some to place the landmarks in the orientation of the celestial constellation of Virgo – thereby seeking the protection of the Virgin Mary for the City. The 'reasoning' revolves around the Capitol on Jenkins Hill, where the Algonquin Tribes held their Grand Councils, while the chiefs of their primary tribe, the Montauk, retained the ancient Egyptian title of 'Pharaoh' – which means Child of the Stars.

Yet amid these conjectures there is the contemporary description of the laying of the cornerstone of the Capitol building in the *Columbian Mirror and Alexandria Gazette* issue of 23 September 1793 which reads: 'The President of the United States pro tem., and the Worshipful Master of No 22, taking their stand to the east of a large stone, and all the Craft forming a circle westward, stood a short time in solemn order.' Certainly when Washington died, he was buried with full Masonic honours, members of Alexandria Lodge No 22 acting as pall-bearers.

It has been alleged that up to 53 of the 56 signatories to the Declaration of Independence were Freemason, as were three of the four in Washington's first Cabinet, 24 of his major-generals and 30 of his 33 brigadiers. These numbers are adduced by some as yet further evidence of a pervasive Masonic influence around Washington's dealings.

It is further conjectured that the design of the Great Seal of the United States incorporates Freemasonic symbolism in depicting an unfinished pyramid surmounted by an eye. But some explanations of its origins run counter to these conclusions, and serve to restore a less sensational (yet perhaps even more fascinating) character to Washington's Christianity.

For example, the unfinished pyramid has its origins on an old colonial bank note designed by Francis Hopkinson, who was in turn consulted in 1780 by the Second Committee of Congress to propose a design for the new Great Seal. The Third Committee in 1782 subsequently adopted it.

Furthermore, instead of the Thompson design on the obverse side of the Great Seal depicting the Phoenix rising in company with 13 stars being some kind of 'illuminati' symbolism connected with the 13 Degrees of Templar initiation, rather it represents in actuality simply the original 13 Colonial States – the subject of Washington's initial wish, in November 1782, to place under the throne and crown of America with Bonnie Prince Charlie as king.

Far stranger, though, is the content of a small book on fencing and duelling entitled *Vindication of the True Art of Self Defence*, written by the Deputy Governor of Edinburgh Castle, Sir William Hope, and published in 1724. A copy was presented to the Library of Congress as late as 1879.[1] The book's curiosity lies not so much in its content, as in what is written in Sir William's hand on the otherwise blank flyleaves.

Here is written a prediction concerning the destiny of the United States, signed and dated 44 years before the outbreak of the Colonial War of Independence: 'Writ at Cornhill, London 1732'. A couple of its predictions will suffice to give a flavour of its apparent accuracy:

> Tis Chaldee says his fate is great
> Whose stars do bear him fortunate.
> Of thy near fate, Amerika,
> I read in stars a prophecy:
> Fourteen divided, twelve the same,
> Sixteen in halfs–each holds a name;
> Four, eight, seven, six–added ten–
> The life line's mark of Four gt. Men ...

This text therefore covers the years 1732 to 1901, during which span Sir William lights upon four great men of 'Amerika' whose combined total in numbers is reached by adding the $4 + 8 + 7 + 6 = 25$ and then adding 10 by creating the third column (i.e. tens). Grand total = 250. At his death Washington was aged 68, Abraham Lincoln 56, Benjamin Harrison 68 and William KcKinley 58. The total of these years is 250.

The next 12 lines predict George Washington's birth and the Colonies' striving for independence:

This day is cradled, far beyond the sea,
One starred by fate to rule both bond and free.
Add double four, thus fix the destined day
When servile knees unbend 'neath freedom's sway
Place six 'fore ten, then read the patriot's name
Whose deeds shall link him to a deathless fame.
Add double four, thus fix the destined day ...

As the prophecy is dated 1732, Washington's date of birth 'beyond the sea' in Virginia, and 44 when added to 1732 gives 1776, we can deduce that it talks of the American Declaration of Independence. Finally, since there are six letters in the name 'George' and ten in 'Washington' it is clear that Washington is the subject of the prophecy.

The prophecy continues in much the same vein, predicting among other great events the assassination of Abraham Lincoln, and concludes with the following four lines that anchor it in history:

These truths prophetic shall completion see Ere time's
deep grave receives the Nineteenth Century!
All planets, stars, twelve signs and horoscope
Attest these certain truths foretold by William Hope.[2]

A descendant of Sir William has added four lines as follows, which serve to introduce the Almighty into the working of the unfolding prophecy thus:

The learned hand that writ these lines no more shall pen for me,
Yet voice shall speak and pulses beat for long posterity
This soul refined through love of kind bewailed life's labors spent,
Then found this truth, his search from youth, Greatness is God's accident.

James Hope

If the work is a forgery, it nevertheless works even as that, for predictions concerning Harrison and McKinley relate to events after the book was acquired by the Library of Congress in 1879. For example, the lines

Then eight 'fore eight a later generation rules,
With light undimmed and shed in progress' school

would refer to the eight letters in the spelling of 'Benjamin' and eight also in 'Harrison', President from 1889 to 1893, his presidency climaxed in the famous Columbian Exposition at Chicago in 1893.

Notes

[1] *A Vindication of the true Act of Self Defence, with a proposal to the honourable members of Parliament for erecting a court of honour in Great Britain, to which is annexed, a short but very useful memorial for swordmen*, Sir William Hope, published in Edinburgh, printed by W. Brown, 1724, Library of Congress Call Number: CR4579.H63.

[2] Source of prophecy text: M.P Hall, *The Secret Destiny of America* (Los Angeles, CA: Philosophical Research Society, 1944; new edn 1991), ch. 14.

three molest in chief argent' and soon afterwards changed to the now familiar 'argent, two bars and three molest in chief gules' – in other words three stars and a couple of horizontal bands. Subsequent members of the family: Lawrence Washington's wife was Margaret Butler, whose Sussex family were descended from the royal Plantagenet line, and in turn whose children entered interesting royal service through one marrying the half-sister of the Duke of Buckingham; another, Thomas Washington, becoming a page to King Charles I, and another, born at Sulgrave in 1602, become the Revd Lawrence Washington who was accused during the English Civil War as a 'malignant royalist' who was 'oft drunk' and removed from his living as Rector of Purleigh. Two sons moved to London and sailed for Virginia in 1656 on the *Sea Horse* of London. His English wife died in America and he remarried the daughter of an American planter, Lieutenant-Colonel Nathaniel Pope, being given as a wedding present the 700-acre estate at Mattox Creek where, in turn, their own son, Lawrence, was born in 1659 – and with him was born the American line of Washingtons of whom George proved to be the means by which the family arms came to evolve into the national flag of the United States of America of which he became President, while his grandmother remained in England and is buried at Whitehaven in Cumbria.

Other influences that bore upon the development of the 'Stars and Stripes' involve inheritance from colonial days, in particular the first collective flag of united colonies known as the 'Continental Colours', 'Great Union Flag' or 'Cambridge Flag', which came into use in 1775 had the British Union Flag in the canton and a field of seven red and six white stripes representing the 13 colonies. The existence of the Union Flag maintained the theory that the colonists still recognized allegiance to the British Crown even as late as 1 January 1776 when it was ceremoniously hoisted by George Washington on Prospect Hill, Somerville, Massachusetts, and by Esek Hopkins's fleet that sailed from Philadelphia three days later. That captured aboard *Lexington* by the British cutter, *Alert* was being flown as late as September 1777, although the Declaration of Independence had occurred on 4 July 1776 and the Congressional resolution describing the new flag had been passed on 14 June 1777 declaring that 'The flag of the united states be thirteen stripes alternate red and white, that the union be thirteen stars white in a blue field representing a new constellation'. As the number of states joining up grew by two with the addition of Vermont and Kentucky in 1795, there seemed to be a good argument for 15 stars and 15 stripes and this was adopted. Curiously this number was maintained throughout the 1812–14 Anglo-American War despite the addition of further new states,[2] until in 1816 a further Congressional resolution permanently reduced the number of stripes back to the old 13, but added the provision for new stars to be added as new states joined up. By 1960 there were 60 stars.

One state flag, that of Hawaii, still retains the Union canton as an inheritance from its days as a British whaling station. Before it became a territory of the United States of America in 1900 under the presidency of McKinley, and later one of the United States themselves in 1959, both the words and music of their national anthem (Hawaii ponoi) were written by King Kalakana (1874–91), following an earlier national anthem written in 1868 by Queen Liliuokalani.

And so, back in August 1814 a British amphibious force sailed into Chesapeake Bay, put ashore, and burned the White House in Washington, DC, in retaliation for the Americans having torched the city of York in British North America. Having captured a number of notables, including Dr William Beanes, the British set their sights on Baltimore, Maryland. British intentions were frustrated by sunken block ships across the bay, shielding gunboats, and the resistance offered by Fort McHenry. On 13 September specialized bomb ketches from which mortar bombs could be fired at the shore were activated by the British and 1,500 bombs, together with Congreve rockets, fell ashore over a period of 25 hours. Only four people were killed and 24 wounded, and with a shore party repulsed at North Point, Baltimore was saved from capture.

Watching all this from a British warship[3] was a lawyer, Francis Scott Key, who was attempting to negotiate the release of the Dr William Beanes who had been captured in Washington during its occupation by the British. Through a scuttle, Key witnessed the bombardment as night fell, fully expecting Baltimore to fall, but the next morning was astonished to see the Stars and Stripes still flying defiantly from Fort McHenry. He was moved to write a poem about it, 'Defence of Fort McHenry'. Set to music and named the 'Star-Spangled Banner', so popular did this turn out to be that it was adopted for official use by the United States Navy in 1889, and became the National Anthem of the United States of America, replacing the 'Hail Columbia', the de facto National Anthem from Washington's time, by Congressional Resolution on 3 March 1931.[4]

The music chosen to accompany the poem had an equally unpredictable origin – in the Anacreontic Societies of London and St Andrews, whose object was to enjoy drinking and promote the art of music. John Stafford Smith composed the music to lyrics written for the societies, and the score was published by Longman and Broderip of London in 1778. A royal association would shortly come about as Smith joined King George III's Chapel Royal at St James's Palace in 1784, becoming Organist of the Chapel Royal from 1802 and Master of the Children from 1805 to 1817. Any rendition of the 'Star-Spangled Banner' in company with successive American Ambassadors invited to the Court at St James's to which they were officially accredited must have been a source of acute embarrassment to King George III – and a mixture of pride and embarrassment to his employee, John Stafford Smith.

The burning of the White House by the British occasioned advice from the elderly Jefferson to President Madison, who was operating temporarily out of the old Post Office in Washington as a result. Jefferson wrote to Dr Thomas Cooper on 10 September 1814: 'The English have burned our Capitol and President's House by means of their force. We can burn down their St. James's and St. Paul's by means of our money, offered to their own incendiaries, of whom there are thousands in London who would do it rather than starve'.[5]

Fortunately, Madison had the foresight to reject the advice.

Notes

1 The earliest extant manuscript of Francis Scott Key's 'Star Spangled Banner' was acquired in 1953 by the Maryland Historical Society, and is located in their H. Furlong Baldwin Library in 2001 West Monument Street, Baltimore, as is one of only two surviving copies of its earliest 1812 broadside printing of the 'Defence of Fort McHenry'.

2 The original flag observed by Key, comprising 15 stars and stripes, is in the collection of the Smithsonian Institution and is on display in the National Museum of American History. It was restored by Amelia Fowler in 1914 and underwent further conservation in 1998.

3 There is dispute as to whether Key was aboard HMS *Minden* or HMS *Surprise* when observing the American flag flying over Fort McHenry following its bombardment. HMS *Minden* was built by Jamshedji Bomanji Wadia in 1810 in Bombay and launched from the Duncan Docks. Christened on 23 June, she saw service not only in Chesapeake Bay in 1812 but also in the bombardment of Algiers, in Java and Australia before ending up as hospital ship in Hong Kong, replacing the shore hospital that had been destroyed in a typhoon. She was replaced by HMS *Alligator* in 1857, sold for scrap and broken up in 1861, leaving as a legacy the names 'Minden Row' and 'Minden Avenue' behind Signal Hill in Kowloon.

4 USA Statute 46, 1508, codified at 36 USC 301.

5 Letter from Thomas Jefferson to Dr Thomas Cooper, printed in *The Writings of Thomas Jefferson*, ed. H.A. Washington (Washington, DC: Taylor and Maury, 1853), vol. 6, pp. 380–1. Jefferson admitted in the same letter that it was 'against the laws of civilized warfare to employ secret incendiaries' but still insisted that a nation was justified in adopting all means to defend itself – in this case 'our money and their pauperism'. Jefferson had in fact predicted in the summer of 1812 that the British would burn a city, but assumed the target would be New York or Boston, expressing his prediction and urging retaliation against London 'not by expensive fleets' but rather 'hired incendiaries' whose hunger 'will make then brave every risk for bread'. Jefferson to General Thaddeus Kosciusko, 3 June 1812, and Jefferson to William Duane, 4 August 1812.

9

Royal Prayer at Times of Personal and National Distress

In times of straits ...
(King James VI of Scotland, 1588, to Queen Elizabeth)[1]

Royal Prayers at Times of National Distress
– Man-made

The Duke of Windsor's Speech at Verdun in May 1939

With the prospect of a second war with Germany looming, the
Duke of Windsor, in May 1939, delivered a speech at what had
been one of the worst scenes of fighting during the First World
War. Although relayed to America, and from there around the
world, the BBC declined to broadcast it and the British press
refused to print it. Its sentiments were evidently heartfelt but
naively out of kilter with the reality of politics and necessary
military preparedness in response to military aggression. The
speech contained the following royal prayer:

> I speak simply as a soldier of the last war whose most earnest
> prayer it is that such a cruel and destructive madness shall
> never again overtake mankind. For two and a half years I have
> deliberately kept out of public affairs, and I still propose to do
> so. I speak for no one but myself, without the previous
> knowledge of any government ... International understanding
> does not always spring spontaneously by itself. There are times
> when it has to be deliberately sought and negotiated and
> political tension is apt to weaken that spirit of mutual
> concession in which conflicting claims can be adjusted ... It

is in the larger interests that peace should be pursued. Somehow I feel that my words tonight will find a sincere echo in all who hear them. It is not for me to put forward concrete proposals – that must be left to those who have the power to guide the nations towards closer understanding. God grant they may accomplish that great task before it is too late.[2]

The Duke had failed, as he later intimated, to keep pace with developments and the true intentions behind the plausible veneer of personalities or to appreciate that the brief peace following the Great War turned out to be, in reality, only a diplomatic interlude before a resumption of military conflict. It was in effect the same war resumed with different weaponry. Churchill and Baldwin could see it coming. Others did not have their foresight or understanding – or wished for a way out by means of appeasement. Hitler's desire to cart the same railway carriage (Wagon-Lits Dining Car 2419) from the old Orient Express rake in which Germany had surrendered on 11 November 1918 to Marshal Foch, to the very same siding in the Forest of Compiègne, 25 miles north-east of Paris, in which that had taken place but this time around to receive the surrender of France on 22 June 1940, and then to have the same carriage blown up in 1945 by an SS unit in Berlin before it could be used for a second surrender of Germany, provides a fascinating insight into Hitler's understanding of what was at stake – and the continuous nature of the conflict stemming from the First World War he was determined to win by means of a Second World War. Perhaps less known is the existence of another Orient Express carriage, yet to undergo restoration, from the rake kept by Hitler in France ready for his intended ceremonial arrival in London.[3]

King George VI's Christmas Day Broadcast in 1939, Britain and France Having Declared War on Germany Three Months Earlier on 3 September

The festival which we know as Christmas is above all the festival of peace and of the home. Among all free peoples the love of peace is profound, for this alone gives security to the home.

But true peace is in the hearts of men, and it is the tragedy of this time that there are powerful countries whose whole direction and policy are based on aggression and the suppression of all that we hold dear for mankind.

It is this that has stirred our peoples and given them a unity unknown in any previous war. We feel in our hearts that we are fighting against wickedness, and this conviction will give us strength from day to day to persevere until victory is assured.

At home we are, as it were, taking the strain for what may lie ahead of us, resolved and confident. We look with pride and thankfulness on the never-failing courage and devotion of the Royal Navy, upon which, throughout the last four months, has burst the storm of ruthless and unceasing war.

And when I speak of our Navy today, I mean all the men of our Empire who go down to the sea in ships, the Mercantile Marine, the mine-sweepers, the trawlers and drifters, from the senior officers to the last boy who has joined up.

To every one in this great Fleet I send a message of gratitude and greeting, from myself as from all my peoples. The same message I send to the gallant Air Force which, in co-operation with the Navy, is our sure shield of defence. They are daily adding laurels to those that their fathers won.

I would send a special word of greeting to the Armies of the Empire, to those who have come from afar, and in particular to the British Expeditionary Force. Their task is hard. They are waiting, and waiting is a trial of nerve and discipline. But I know that when the moment comes for action they will prove themselves worthy of the highest traditions of their great Service.

And to all who are preparing themselves to serve their country, on sea or land or in the air, I send my greeting at this time. The men and women of our far-flung Empire working in their several vocations, with the one same purpose, all are members of the great Family of Nations which is prepared to sacrifice everything that freedom of spirit may be saved to the world.

Such is the spirit of the Empire; of the great Dominions, of India, of every Colony, large or small. From all alike have come offers of help, for which the Mother Country can never be sufficiently grateful. Such unity in aim and in effort has never been seen in the world before.

I believe from my heart that the cause which binds together my peoples and our gallant and faithful Allies is the cause of Christian civilisation. On no other basis can a true civilisation be built.

Let us remember this through the dark times ahead of us and when we are making the peace for which all men pray.

A new year is at hand. We cannot tell what it will bring. If it brings peace, how thankful we shall all be. If it brings us continued struggle we shall remain undaunted.

In the meantime I feel that we may all find a message of encouragement in the lines which, in my closing words, I would like to say to you: 'I said to the man who stood at the Gate of the Year, "Give me a light that I may tread safely into the unknown". And he replied, "Go out into the darkness, and put your hand into the Hand of God. That shall be to you better than light, and safer than a known way".'

May that Almighty Hand guide and uphold us all.[4]

'Prier for men to saie entering battayle', 1544

King George VI's prayer for the British Expeditionary Force in 1939, about to encounter hostilities in enemy occupied France, had a forbear 400 years earlier in the form of Queen Katherine Parr's 'Praier for men to saie entering battayle', composed in the summer of 1544 as King Henry VIII joined his troops in France at the siege of Boulogne, leaving Katherine behind on the other side of the English Channel as Queen Regent:

> O Almighty Kynge and lorde of hostes
> Which by the angelles thereunto apoynted
> Doost minister both warre and peace,
> And whiche diddest geve unto David
> Bothe courage and strength
> Beying but a littell one,
> Unarmed, and unexpert in feates of warre
> With his slinge to sette upon and overthrowe
> The great huge Goliath:
> Our cause now being just,
> And beying inforced to entre into warre and battaile,
> We most humbly beseech thee
> (O Lorde of hostes)

so to tourne the hertes of our enemies
to the desire of peace,
that no christen bloud be spilt,
or lese graunt (O Lorde)
that with small effusion of bloud,
and to the little hurte and damoge of innocents,
we maie to thy glorie obteine victorie:
and that the warres beyne sone ended,
we maie al with one herte and mynde,
knitte together in concord and unitie,
laude and praise thee;
which lyvest and reignest,
worlde without ende.
Amen.[5]

This was first published as one of a corpus of five prayers printed at the end of Katherine Parr's *Prayers or Medytacions*, published in 1545. It was written at the same time, during the war in France, as Cranmer was composing his new Litany, and may have been intended to complement the new vernacular services, if not actually to be included.

Princess Elizabeth's Broadcast to the Commonwealth, 13 October 1940

Princess Elizabeth made her first public speech on 13 October 1940, in a radio broadcast to the children of the Commonwealth, many of them evacuees billeted far away from home as the Second World War unfolded, and ended with the observation that the Almighty would lend protection:

> In wishing you all 'good evening' I feel that I am speaking to friends and companions who have shared with my sister and myself many a happy Children's Hour.
>
> Thousands of you in this country have had to leave your homes and be separated from your fathers and mothers. My sister Margaret Rose and I feel so much for you as we know from experience what it means to be away from those we love most of all.
>
> To you, living in new surroundings, we send a message of true sympathy and at the same time we would like to thank the

kind people who have welcomed you to their homes in the country.

All of us children who are still at home think continually of our friends and relations who have gone overseas – who have travelled thousands of miles to find a wartime home and a kindly welcome in Canada, Australia, New Zealand, South Africa and the United States of America.

My sister and I feel we know quite a lot about these countries. Our father and mother have so often talked to us of their visits to different parts of the world. So it is not difficult for us to picture the sort of life you are all leading, and to think of all the new sights you must be seeing, and the adventures you must be having.

But I am sure that you, too, are often thinking of the Old Country. I know you won't forget us; it is just because we are not forgetting you that I want, on behalf of all the children at home, to send you our love and best wishes – to you and to your kind hosts as well.

Before I finish I can truthfully say to you all that we children at home are full of cheerfulness and courage. We are trying to do all we can to help our gallant sailors, soldiers and airmen, and we are trying, too, to bear our own share of the danger and sadness of war.

We know, everyone of us, that in the end all will be well; for God will care for us and give us victory and peace. And when peace comes, remember it will be for us, the children of today, to make the world of tomorrow a better and happier place.

My sister is by my side and we are both going to say goodnight to you.

Come on, Margaret.

Goodnight, children.

Goodnight, and good luck to you all.[6]

Wartime National Days of Prayer

The royal family had their share of narrow escapes as the Second World War unfolded. The Domestic Chapel in Buckingham Palace, where King George VI had been at prayer just two hours before, was bombed and destroyed by the Luftwaffe on 13 September 1940.[7] Buckingham Palace was targeted nine times,

The King Prayed Here 2 Hours Before Bombing

This was the Royal Chapel at Buckingham Palace.
Only two hours before a Nazi bomb crashed through the roof and caused the havoc this picture reveals, our King was kneeling here in prayer.

War damage to Domestic Chapel, Buckingham Palace, inflicted by Luftwaffe raid on 13 September 1940. Sunday Pictorial, September 1940

and sustained much damage. But the attempt on 15 September 1940 was frustrated by a Royal Air Force (RAF) pilot, Ray Holmes, who, having run out of ammunition, decided to ram the German bomber in flight. Both planes crashed and the whole engagement was captured on film. The German plane's engine was retrieved and displayed at the Imperial War Museum, and following the War, Mr Holmes was appointed a King's Messenger, dying at the age of 90 in 2005.

The 1940 National Day of Prayer

Initially, in April 1940, the Archbishop of Canterbury declined to set aside a special day of prayer, on the grounds that it would be 'misunderstood or rather misrepresented by the enemy', but by May the Archbishop was leading the National Day of Prayer at Westminster Abbey. In the Empire's dark hour, the King himself had proclaimed a Day of National Prayer throughout the Empire.

The BBC broadcast three services, one of them conducted by the Archbishop of York, to Britain's Forces of the Crowns. In Westminster Cathedral, Cardinal Kinsley celebrated High Mass. King's Chaplain, the Revd Pat McCormick, preached at the London Coliseum. Lord Nuffield encouraged every munitions worker to take for his text on Sunday: 'Work and pray'.

In Egyptian mosques Moslems were exhorted by their holy leaders to prepare for a 'Jihad' to help the Allied cause. On the desert near Cairo, Indian Moslems created 'prayer grounds' decorated with chromium-plated bottle caps, and prayed for the Allied cause.

On May 23, the King, political leaders and newspaper editors issued a call for a 'National Day of Prayer' to be held on Sunday, 26 May. On 24 May 1940, Allied soldiers were trapped hopelessly on the beaches of Dunkirk, awaiting apparently certain anihilation. No one could have anticipated what was to happen during the subsequent three days. Twenty-four hours after the call for prayer, Adolf Hitler inexplicably ordered a halt to operation Sealion.[8] Two days later, on 26 May, the nation gathered to pray. Church attendance increased hugely on the day, and included an emormous gathering at Westminster Abbey during which the congregation prayed for the British Forces under attack at Dunkirk.

In his dairy Neville Chamberlain wrote: 'May 26. Blackest day of all ... This was the National Day of Prayer.' Following the fall of Boulgogne and Calais to the Nazis during the day, forcing the British Expeditionary Force (BEF) to fall back on Dunkirk, at seven o'clock that same evening the order was issued to attempt a seaborne evacuation of Dunkirk with an appeal to assemble 'little ships' of light draft to muster in perparation in Southern ports to mount an armada capable of evacuating troops surrounded at Dunkirk.

Under the protection of gunfire from the Royal Navy and fighter aircraft of the RAF, the evacuation of Dunkirk shared by the little ships turned into a miraculously successful endeavour (Operation 'Dynamo), against all the odds.

The initial plans involved evacuating 45,000 men of the BEF over a two-day period under the direction of Vice-Admiral B.H. Ramsey. But during the next five days Operation Dynamo was expanded to rescue from the Dunkirk beaches 8,000 men on the 27 May, 18,000 on the 28th, 47,000 on the 29th, 54,000 on the 30th and 68,000 on the 31st – all carried to Britain – a total of 195,000, both British and French. Every phase of the operation was subject to heavy air, sea and land attack. Forty British, six French and a Polish destroyer took part, together with 800 other vessels, large and small. Losses were very considerable, with the evacuation continuing into early June.

Revisionist historians find such facts hard to swallow. One as recently as 2004 went so far on the BBC's Home History website as to claim:

> Increasingly concerned at the air of unreality that seemed to permeate Britain, on 4th June Churchill addressed the House of Commons in terms that spelt out clearly the truly desperate nature of Britain's situation. He reminded his countrymen that wars were not won by evacuations, and that 'what has happened in France and Belgium is a colossal military disaster'. But the British people didn't really believe him; they much preferred the myth to the reality, and they were not prepared to listen to anyone who sought to puncture their belief, not even Churchill himself. They were a difficult people to feed on lies, but they were perfectly happy to lie to themselves, particularly when that lie held the key to their survival as a nation.[9]

This 'revisionist' slur on the efforts of the nation's corporate prayer is dismissed by the evidence of those who fought and were rescued from the beaches at Dunkirk, and the surviving crews of the many little ships that made that it possible, and the Royal Navy survivors of the sequence of events that culminated in Operation Dynamo. That revisionist historians should, in the face of the chronological facts, feel the need to attack the efficacy of prayer at times of such distress may say as much about the state of denial of those who propound such views as the central role of prayer in the lives of those it physically affected.

The 1941 National Day of Prayer

The official form for the National Day of Prayer in 1941 printed a prayer 'by Sir Francis Drake' – an attribution only partially correct but that was to stick. Although the Revd Philip Nichols was Drake's Chaplain aboard his ship, and might have been expected to have recorded any prayer composed by Drake himself, 'Drake's Prayer' was in fact extrapolated centuries later from a text within a letter Captain Drake wrote to Queen Elizabeth's Secretary of State, Francis Walsingham, on board the 'Elizabeth Bonaventure' lying at anchor at Cape Sagres on 17 May 1587 after 'singeing the King of Spain's beard' by sacking Sagres: 'There must be a begynnyng of any great matter, but the contenewing unto the end untyll it be thoroughly ffynyshed yeldes the trew glory.'[10]

In a collection of prayers of early times compiled by Eric Milner-White, Dean of York, and published by the Oxford University Press in 1941, the words of Drake were adapted to produce the following text used as 'Drake's Prayer' for the National day of Prayer in 1941:

> O Lord God, when thou givest to Thy servants to endeavour any great matter, grant us also to know that it is not the beginning, but the continuing of the same unto the end, until it be thoroughly finished, which yieldeth the true glory; through Him that for the finishing of Thy work laid down His life, our Redeemer, Jesus Christ.

It was included in *A Naval Prayer Book* that became an Admiralty Book of Reference, but in 1965 this 'BR' was superseded by *Pray With the Navy* by Leonard Lewis Griffiths, now known in the Royal Navy as 'BR 426', available to chaplains and commanding officers.

Drake's Prayer was employed by the Chaplain of The Fleet during the marriage service of HRH The Duke of York with Miss Sarah Ferguson in Westminster Abbey on Wednesday 23 July, 1986. Upon this occasion Drake's Prayer was redolent with the Duke's recent Royal Naval helicopter operations during the Falklands War in 1982.

By the time of the next National Day of Prayer in 1942 the spontaneity of the concept had worn thin in the eyes of some.

Sir Alan 'Tommy' Lascelles, Assistant Private Secretary to King George VI, recorded in his diary that:

> it seems to me an insult to any civilized Deity to imagine that he is affected, one way of the other, by mass-production prayers, decreed by government – which is all these national days really are. Moreover it is an insult to all of us also; every decent man has 'prayed' many times on each day and night during the last three years, of his own initiative and without any stimulus from the temporal powers. I prefer to think that such prayers, however brief and humble, are more likely to touch the heart of the Immanent Will than any herd demonstration. But I am confessedly an oclophile in all matters relating to man's relations with God. In which I am, to some extent, supported by the authority of St. Chrysosotom (who admits two or three to be a representative gathering).[11]

Lascelles was making this observation while attending upon the King in Crathie Church, and accompanied by Grand Duchess Xenia Alexandrovna (1875–1960), sister of Tsar Nicholas II, who had been rescued from Yalta along with other Romanovs and brought to Britain aboard HMS *Marlborough* and was living in Craigowan for the duration of the Second World War.

Prayers of National Distress – Natural Disasters

Royal Prayers for the Boxing Day Tsunami, 2004

The Queen and other members of the royal family, as members of the congregation at St Mary's, Sandringham, joined in prayers for what has turned out to be a death toll of over 300,000 victims of the tsunami that struck the Indian Ocean on Boxing Day 2004 as a result of an undersea earthquake.

At the service the Revd Jonathan Riviere led the prayers, and the Bishop of Norwich, the Rt Revd Graham James, preached that he had been scarcely able to believe what he had seen and heard during the week's coverage of the tsunami, but made the pertinent observation that 'a wall of water 30ft or more high travelling at several hundred miles an hour' and creating such unimaginable devastation raised difficult theological questions. Although 'words seem cheap when the cost of lives have been so expensive' he had concluded that: 'God has given us an earth that lives and moves. It is not inert, it is alive – that is why we can live. A living and moving earth has its dangers. Christianity never avoids the darker side of human existence.'

Queen Elizabeth I was faced with similar theological questions 424 years earlier when a massive earthquake under the English Channel struck terror into the Southern Counties and Northern France.

Queen Elizabeth's Earthquake Prayer, 1580

A Prayer to be used of all householders, with their whole family, every evening before they go to bed, that it would please God to turn his wrath from us, threatened in the last terrible earthquake.

Set forth by authority.

Oh eternal, mighty, and most loving Father, which hast no desire of the death of a sinner, but that he convert and live, and unto whom nothing is so pleasant as the repentant, contrite and sorrowful heart of a penitent person: for thou art that kind Father that fallest most lovingly upon the neck of the lost son, kissest, embracest and feastest him, when he returneth from the puddle of pleasures and swill of the swine, and disdainest not the repentant prayer of thy poor and sinful servants, whensoever with true faith they return and call upon thee, as we have most comfortable examples in David, Manasses, Magdalene, Peter, and the thief upon the gibbet: we most heartily and humbly beseech thy fatherly goodness, to look down from the throne of thy mercy-seat upon us most miserable and sinful slaves of Satan, which with fearful and trembling hearts do quake and shake at the strange and terrible token of thy wrath and indignation appearing most evidently to us, by the shaking and moving of the earth, which is thy footstool; whereby (if we be not destitute of grace) we be warned that thy coming down amongst us, to visit our sins in most terrible manner, can not be far off, seeing thou treadest so hard upon thy footstool the earth, which we most shamefully have polluted and defiled with our wicked, sinful, and rebellious lives, notwithstanding thy continual and calling upon us by thy servants, the Prophets and preachers, by whom we have learned to know thy will, but have not followed it; we have heard much and done little, yea, nothing at all; but like most perverse and unthankful children have made a mock of thy word, derided thy ministers, and accounted thy threatenings trifles, and thy warnings of no weight or moment: wherefore we have justly deserved to taste most deeply of the bitter cup of thy anger and vengeance, by wars, famine, pestilence, yea, and eternal death, if thou shouldest not temper the rigour of thy justice with the mildness of thy mercy. But such is thy fatherly affection towards us, that thou shewest thyself slow to anger, long suffering, and of much patience and mercy. Yea thou art a thousand times more ready to forget and forgive than we ask and require forgiveness. Therefore though we be not worthy of the least mite of thy mercy, yet, gracious Lord, look not upon us and our sins, but upon thy own self and thy son Jesus Christ, the fountain of grace, the treasure of mercy, the salve of all sickness, the jewel of Joy, and the only haven of succour and safety: by him we come to thee, in him and for him we trust to find that we have lost, and gain that he hath got: he is the scale of Jacob, by whom we climb up to thee, and thou by the Angels of thy mercy comest down to us: him we present unto thee, and not ourselves, his death and not our doings, his bloody wounds and not our detestable deservings, whose merits are so great, as thy mercy can not be little, and our ransom so rich, that our beggarly and beastly sins are noting in thy sight, for the great pleasure and satisfaction that thou takest of his pains and passion. Turn this Earthquake, O Lord, to the benefit of thine elect, as thou didst when thou shookest the prison, loosedst the locks, fetters and chains of thy servants, Paul and Silas, and broughtest them out of prison, and converted their keeper: so, gracious Lord, strike the hearts of thy tyrants with the terror of this thy work, that they may know that they are but men, and that thou art Sampson, that for their mocking and spiting of thee and thy word can shake the pillars of their palaces, and throw them upon the furious Philistines' heads. Turn thy wrath, O Lord, from thy children that call upon thy Name, to the conversion or confusion of thine enemies that defy and abhor thy Name, and deface thy glory. Thou hast knocked long at their doors, but they will not open to let thee in: burst open therefore the brazen gates of their stony hearts, thou that art able of stones to raise up children to Abraham: and, finally, so touch our hearts with the finger of thy grace, that we may deeply muse upon our sinful lives, to amend them, and call for thy mercy to forgive and pardon them, through Christ our Lord, who liveth with thee, and the Holy Ghost, three persons and one eternal God, to whom be all dominion and glory, with praise and thanksgiving, for ever and ever, Amen.[12]

The Earthquake Prayer was issued by Queen Elizabeth I's royal command 'set forth by authority ... Imprinted at London by Christopher Barker Printer to the Queene's Majestie 1580. Cum Privilegio'.

This earthquake was felt throughout England and Flanders. A recent study undertaken during the construction of the Channel Tunnel concluded that the 1580 earthquake had a magnitude of 5.3 to 5.9 with its epicentre located beneath the Channel in the Dover Straits at a focal depth of 20–25 km.

At the time, sailors in the English Channel were overwhelmed by freak waves and swells that sank more than 24 English, French and Flemish vessels. A passenger on a boat from Dover reported that his ship had grounded on the seabed five times and that the waves had been taller than the masts of ships.

Unlike England where the quake lasted a minute or so, in Boulogne and Calais it lasted a quarter of an hour and was followed by a 'deluge' (tsunami) that swamped the town and surrounding countryside, drowning both cattle and people, with parts of both town walls collapsing.

Further from the coast, furniture danced on the floors and wine casks rolled around. The belfry at Notre Dame de Lorette, together with several buildings at Lille, collapsed. Stones fell from buildings in Arras, Douai, Bethune and Rouen. At Pontoise Cathedral the windows cracked and blocks of stone dropped from its vaulted roof. The bells at Beauvais rang by themselves.

In Flanders chimneys fell and cracks opened in the city walls of Ghent and Oudenarde. Peasants in the fields reported a low rumble and saw the ground roll in waves.

On the English side of the Channel, sections of wall fell in Dover and a landslip opened and altered the look of the white cliffs. At Sandwich a loud noise was heard from the Channel as church arches cracked and the gable end of the transept at St Peter's Church fell down. In Hythe, Saltwood Castle, notable as the site where the plot to assasinate Thomas Becket was hatched in December 1170, was rendered uninhabitable until it was repaired in the nineteenth century.

In London, half a dozen chimney stacks came down including a pinnacle on Westminster Abbey, and two children were killed by stones falling from the roof of Christ's Church Hospital. In looking for an explanation, some Puritans pinned the blame as God's retribution upon the emerging theatre scene of the time in London, deemed by some to represent the work of the devil.

Elsewhere stones fell from Ely Cathedral and part of Stratford Castle in Essex collapsed, while in Scotland reports of the quake there disturbed the young James VI, whose informants also described it as the work of the devil.

There were aftershocks. Before dawn the next morning, between 4 p.m. and 5 p.m. further houses collapsed near Dover, and a second tsunami was reported to have drowned 120 people. A spate of further aftershocks was noticed in east Kent on 1–2 May.

In 'A Discourse containing many wonderful examples of God's Indignation poured upon divers people for their intolerable sins, which treatise may be read instead of some part of the Homily, where there is no sermon', a chronicle is made of

> the strange things that befell in the Realm of Naples in the year 1566 ... the Earthquake, whereby a great part of the City of Ferrera in Italy was destroyed in the year 1570 ... the miraculous sights that were seen in France about Montpellier the year 1573 ... the like terrible sight ... at Prague, and the wonderful new Star so long time fixed in Heaven [November 1572, brighter than Jupiter the star stood in Cassiopea's chair for 16 months], great and strange fashioned lights in the firmament at night times [14 and 15 November 1574 according to Stowe], culminating in the 1580 Earthquake.

Because 'it could not have been in so many places universally at one instant both by sea and land' and was preceded by no tokens ... as ... troubledness of water even in the deepest wells ... and great and terrible sounds in the earth ... we may well conclude ... that this miracle proceeded not of the course of any natural causes, but of God's only determinate purpose.[13]

The famous 'earthquake letter' from Gabrial Harvey to Edmund Spencer mocked both popular and academic methods of accounting for the tremors which fell during Easter week. There is also contemporary reference to the 1580 earthquake in Shakespeare's *Romeo and Juliet*, which also serves to date the play to 1591: '*Nurse*: "Tis since the earthquake now eleven years'.[14]

The British Geological Survey (BGS) routinely monitors UK earthquakes around the clock, and the fact that they occur almost daily throughout the UK and its territorial waters, though only a few prove to be structurally significant, means that the theological question, coupled with the Sovereign's duty and concern for the welfare of the realm, ought to remain current for the next serious manifestation. A recent example, typical of the observations received by the BGS on 2008, was officially recorded as follows:

> BGS have received a report from a resident in West Loch, Tarbert, Argyll & Bute, of an event on 9 August at approximately 13:35 BST (12:35 UTC). The report described 'the house shook' and 'various objects rattled'. The resident also confirmed that 'it was the talk of the local hotel as the earthquake had been felt by many Tarbert residents' and that 'it was also felt by others in Lochgilphead'.

British Geological Survey data for a 30-day period subsequent to this report in the months of August–September, 2008, give a representative sample of UK earthquakes for any given period of 30 days:

22nd Aug: Port Appin, Argyll/Bute (Magnitude 1.2)
23rd Aug: North West France (Magnitude 2.6)
23rd Aug: Southern Norway (Magnitude 2.8)
27th Aug: Offshore North West France (Magnitude 1.7)
29th Aug: 35 KM East of Helmsdale, Moray Firth (Magnitude 0.9)

30th Aug: 8 KM South West of Southport, Irish Sea
(Magnitude 1.6)

5th Sept: Dumfries (Magnitude 1.1)

8th Sept: Isle of Mull (Magnitude 1.3)

10th Sept: 10 KM SSW of Brecon, Powys (Magnitude 1.4)

12th Sept: Cumnock, East Ayrshire (Magnitude 1.3)

18th Sept: KM South East of Bridgewater (Magnitude 1.2)

19th Sept: Northwest France (offshore) (Magnitude 1.8)

The earthquake occurring 1 km east of Folkestone on 28 April 2007 was measured at less than 5 km below the surface. At 4.2 magnitude, it proved to be the highest recorded intensity (at 6 on the European Microseismic Scale) for a British earthquake in over 100 years. It constituted the largest earthquake in the United Kingdom since a 4.4 magnitude occurrence in 1950. On average, earthquakes of magnitude 4.2 occur in the United Kingdom mainland every five years. That which struck the Straits of Dover in 1776 was very significant, and even that which struck Dudley in the West Midlands in 2002, measuring 4.7, was felt widely across England and Wales.

Royal Prayer in the Modern Age of Disaster Prevention

The upshot of understanding better the geophysical, meteor-ological and astronomical forces involved in such natural disasters is that the theology underlying public royal prayer at such times of distress and emergency needs also to absorb this greater understanding of the world around us.

The Sovereign has often been at the cutting edge of such understanding. The Queen launched the modern age of United Kingdom nuclear power on 17 October 1956 when opening Calder Hall in 1956, standing in the shadow of the massive chimneys of the Windscale plant, where explosives were made for Britain's first atomic bomb, and alluded to the origin of that technology when remarking: 'This new power, which has proved itself to be such a terrifying weapon of destruction is harnessed for the first time for the common good of our community.'

The enduring safety of this technology is always threatened

by such massive forces as earthquakes or human error in its care, and the likelihood of a nuclear accident with fatal consequential nuclear fallout is only a matter of time, elsewhere if not in the United Kingdom. Windscale, Three Mile Island and Chernobyl have all fallen victim to accidents.

Fields previously understood as in realms only of God, now fall to the hands of man as his instrument. Nuclear fallout approaching the shores of the United Kingdom might be tackled effectively out at sea by a Royal Navy peacetime role delivering (by shell or missile) silver iodide crystals for glaciogenic cloud seeding (the most likely form in Northern climes) and salt crystals for warm cloud hygroscopic cloud seeding – technology already applied by aircraft and artillery shells in other areas of the globe to encourage crop growth. Its all too effective aerial application in the Bristol Channel during 'operation cumulus' before the force of its likely consequences was properly understood, led to the tragic consequence of the flash flooding of Lynmouth in 1952 by a deluge of 90 million tonnes of water, causing 35 deaths. The criticism was that, in playing with the weather, man was playing God, but now technology has moved on into the nuclear, biological and chemical age, and the consequence of not applying such 'God-like' technology to induce rainfall out at sea in times of nuclear crises will lead to yet greater suffering.

The Ocean Weather Service can provide data that begins to question the modern relevance of such biblical sayings as John 3.8: 'The wind bloweth where it listeth, and thou hearest the sound thereof, but canst not tell whence it cometh, and whither it goeth, so is everyone that is born of the spirit.' Queen Elizabeth I attributed the action of great winds that dispersed the Spanish Armada to the intentions of the Almighty in 1588 in a letter to King James VI of Scotland:

> To my very good brother the king of Scots. Now may appear, my dear bother, how malice joined with might strikest to make a shameful end to a villainous beginning, for by God's singular favour, having their fleet well beaten in the narrow seas and pressing with all violence to achieve some watering place to continue their pretended invasion, the winds have carried

them to your coasts, where I doubt not they shall receive small succour and less welcome ... Elizabeth R.[15]

Yet there are now methods to control and direct wind to the extent that royal prayer invoking divine blessing upon such technology has meant that theology as expressed through royal prayer has had to keep pace with such advances, and with it also the blame should it go wrong.

In other words the royal prayers are at the very forefront of advancing civilization and exploration of the unknown, and with it increased understandings of the workings of the Almighty.

The royal family has christened nuclear submarines with prayer, but instead of their defensive role in war, they also include the possibility that Trident II D5 submarine-launched missiles could carry this 'civil defence' capability, and would be especially valuable if the nuclear plume were considered too potent for approach by a surface fleet. Since only four thermo-nuclear warheads are permitted currently to be carried aboard each of the 16 missiles aboard strategic submarine, ballistic nuclear (SSBN) vessels, it might prove a particularly useful adjunct to their capabilities to fit some with cloud seeding warheads, especially as the range of 12,000 km would allow the Royal Navy to begin to tackle a nuclear fallout problem a long way off, to the benefit of numerous nations, including the United Kingdom.[16]

Control of air flow and the development of powered flight have also led to increased use of this knowledge throughout the twentieth century. The invention and development of the hovercraft by Sir Christopher Cockerell is an example of frontier technology employing the harnessing of wind thrust. So nonplussed were the government authorities in 1956 that they immediately placed an order for the invention to be classified as 'secret' and then filed away, only to release it for development a year later as overseas competitors began to catch up. The royals were intimately associated with its advancement.

In 1959 the Saunders Roe Nautical One (SRN1) was launched at Cowes, and the Duke of Edinburgh 'flew' it shortly afterwards at such speed that the sea dented its bows. This was known as the 'royal dent' and was subsequently retained in the 'hull' as a symbol of royal approval. The designs of hovercraft became larger until the largest of all, the SRN4, capable of carrying 254 passengers and 30 cars, was named the 'Mountbatten Class'. On 31 July 1969 Princess Margaret christened one in her name, as did Princess Anne on 8 August and, most recently, the Duke of Edinburgh christened the *Solent Express* at the Duver, St Helens, Isle of Wight, on 24 July 2006. The technology has spread around the globe, and all manner of uses for it are to be seen. After a certain quandary as to whether hovercraft were ships or aeroplanes, Canadians and other nations formed the opinion that they were ships, not aircraft, hence the form of rubric employed when the Canadian Coast Guard hovercraft *Siyay* was christened on 5 September 2000 by Mrs Herb Dhaliwal at Coast Guard Station Sea Island, Richmond, British Columbia: 'I christen this ship *Siyay*, and may God bless her and all those that sail in her' said Mrs Dhaliwal, wife of the Hon. Herb Dhaliwal, Minister of Fisheries and Oceans Canada, MP for Vancouver South-Burnaby, who represented the Government of Canada at the naming and dedication of the vessel. The tradition of inviting ladies to become 'Godmothers' of ships was employed at the christenings of hovercraft too. Thus Mary Wilson, wife of Prime Minister Harold Wilson, found herself christening Hoverlloyd's *Swift* on 29 January 1969.

On a much faster scale, soon after Concorde was first flown on 2 March 1969, the Duke of Edinburgh took the controls during a two-hour supersonic flight of Concorde 002 on 12 January 1972, thereby placing the royal family at the forefront of understanding and handling modern technology, with which prayer would have to keep pace.

Notes

[1] Letter from King James VI of Scotland to Queen Elizabeth, 1 August 1588 beginning 'In times of straits true friends are tried', British Library MS Additional 23240, art.23, fol. 75r. As James was writing this letter, the Spanish Armada, prevented from landing by the

English, was heading up the North Sea toward the coast of Scotland 'whereby your adversaries may have ado not with England but with the whole Isle of Britain'.

2   J. Bryan, III,and J.V. Murphy, *The Windsor Story* (London: Granada, 1979

3   S. Sherwood, *Venice Simplon Orient Express – The Worlds's Most Celebrated Train* 4th edn (London: Weidenfeld and Nicolson, 1996), p. 73.

4   Royal Archives, Windsor Castle.

5   'Prayers or Meditacions, wherein the mind is stirred paciently to suffre all afflictions here, to sette at naught the vaine prosperitie of this worlde, and alwaie to long for the everlastynge felicitee: collected out of certayne holy woorkes by the most virtuous and gracious Princes Catharine, Quene of Englande, France and Ireland, Imprinted at London: Fletestrete, in the hous of Thomas Bethelette, Anno Dni 1545', British Library, Catalogue System Number 000634813, Shelf Mark G.11660. The BL conjectures an original date of 1540 for elements of the content.

6   BBC Written Archives (and BBC Audio Clips Library where the item is catalogued deficiently as 'HRH Princess Elizabeth sends message to the children of Great Britain').

7   *Sunday Pictorial*, September 1940, interior photographs of the almost total destruction of the Domestic Chapel and detailed text headed 'The King Prayed here 2 Hours Before Bombing'. Archive of HM Chapel Royal, St James's Palace.

8   Liddell Hart Centre for Military Archives, King's College London, catalogued as Liddell: 15/15/11 [1947] 'Papers from German sources relating to the Battle of Britain and Operation SEA-LION in 1940, including transcripts of directives and orders issued by Adolf Hitler, FM Wilhelm Keitel, Gen Alfred Jodl and Reichsmarschall Hermann Göring, Jun–Oct 1940, and proposals by Gen Schmid of the German Air Force Operations Staff (Intelligence) for the conduct of air warfare against Britain, dated 22 Nov 1939; extracts from OKW's directives for military administration of Britain, 1940; analysis of an interview in Jun 1945 with Gen Erhard Milch, former Director-General of Aircraft Production, and Gen Adolf Galland, former Commander in Chief Luftwaffe Fighter Arm. 1 file'.

9   Published on the BBC website, 6 February 2004.

10 'Newes out of the coast of Spaine, The true Report of the honourable service for England, performed by Sir F. Drake in ... April and May ... 1587', British Library, Shelf Mark G.6512 (1).

11 *King's Counsellor – Abdication and War: The Diaries of Sir Alan Lascelles*,
     ed. D. Hart-Davis (London: Weidenfeld and Nicolson, 2006), diary
     entry 3 September 1942.
12 Cambridge University Library, Special Forms of Prayer General 1580;
     British Library, Shelf Mark 3504.bb.19, System Number 002196643;
     also printed in *Liturgies and Occasional Forms of Prayer set forth in the
     Reign of Queen Elizabeth*, ed. Revd Keatinge Clay, The Parker Society
     (Cambridge: Cambridge University Press, 1847), pp. 564–6.
13 MS Williams, Cambridge University Library; and printed in *Liturgies
     and Occasional Forms of Prayer set forth in the Reign of Queen Elizabeth*,
     ed. Revd Keatinge Clay, The Parker Society (Cambridge: Cambridge
     University Press, 1847), pp. 568–75.
14 W. Skakespeare, *Romeo and Juliet*, I.iii, l. 22.
15 British Library, Additional Manuscript 23240, art.24, fol.77, with
     remnants of seal and ribbon still attached.
16 Author's correspondence with the Meteorological Office and Her
     Majesty's Armed Forces from April 1986.

10

Royal Prayers under Revolution

Prayers of the Russian Royal Family

On a purely personal level between family relatives, royal prayer is central to practical action over concern for the sick. In the case of Grand Duchess Olga's anxiety for her mother there survives the following prayer written on board a Russian Imperial Yacht on 3 April 1912 and sent to her mother at the new Imperial White Palace at Livadia on the slope of Mount Moghabi facing Yalta on the Black Sea:

> Precious Mama, God bless you and help you not to be too sad. It is awful to be on our beloved yacht without its 'sunshine' who we will miss frightfully. I should so much prefer to remain here with you than being on board without you. May He make you well again and then everything will be all right. It must be very hard for you too, sweet love, but God will reward you for your sorrow. Good night. All prayers and thoughts remain with you. Good night. I kiss you lovingly and remain your ever very true loving daughter Olga.[1]

Olga was the eldest daughter of the Tsar and Tsarina, born at Tsarskoye Selo Palace on 3 November 1895, and was to be martyred along with the rest of the Imperial family by the Bolsheviks.

But in 1912 she was writing her prayer aboard one of the two Imperial Royal Yachts. The old *Poliarnaia Zvesda* (Pole Star), built by the Baltiiski Shipbuilding Company and launched at St Petersburg in 1888, was a steam yacht whose main use was for the Empress Marie Fedorovna and her five children. The yearly court round included the family's return each summer to the old palace at Peterhof, and an annual cruise in the Baltic aboard the

Poliarnaia Zvesda to rendezvous with the Swedish royal family for a gathering of royal yachts in the Baltic, with youngsters housed ashore in chalets on the royal estate. This provided a rare occasion for Alexander III to relax with his family away from the genuine fear of an assassin's bomb or bullet. A cow was always numbered among the crew of this vessel and sailed with them to provide fresh milk for the royal children. In 1894 the *Poliarnaia Svesda* had sailed to England with Nicholas II aboard on his mission of betrothal to Queen Victoria's granddaughter, Princess Alix of Hesse-Darmsradt, who was to become his Empress Alexandra Federovna. A year later, in 1895, a new Russian Imperial Yacht was built by Burmeister and Wain in Copenhagen, and launched with the name *Standart*.

Standart was the biggest royal yacht at the time, and is notable for incorporating a Russian Orthodox chapel in addition to the usual the state rooms.[2] The chapel was arranged in a semi-circle around one of the masts that passed through the deck, and contained both large and small icons mounted into a wooden panelled iconstasis. Whenever *Standart* went to sea the Orthodox Holy Synod appointed a chaplain to conduct daily divine office

Russian Imperial Yacht Standart in 1896

for royal family and crew. As well as being used for family purposes, *Standart* hosted a wealth of fascinating events, including the departure of the Russian Fleet to sail around the globe to engage the Japanese in the Far East, meetings with the German Kaiser, and visits to Cowes Week off the Isle of Wight,[3] at one of which the Tsar reviewed the assembled British Royal Navy. She was even the inspiration behind a Fabergé egg of the same name produced in 1907. The Imperial family was aboard *Standart* when news of the assassination of Archduke Ferdinand at Sarajevo came through.

Following the murder of the Imperial family by the Bolsheviks the *Poliarnaia Svesda* had her stokers' quarters used to confine the Tsarina's confidante, Anna Vyrubova, and later served as a training ship for stokers in the Second World War. *Standart* had a spectacular career ahead of her. While at Kronstadt on the outskirts of St Petersberg (Petrograd) her crew took part in the 1917 February Revolution which culminated in the rise of the Provisional Government, the toppling of the Tsar on 2 March (Julian Calendar), and then the formation of the Tsentrobalt on 30 April, being the Bolshevik organization of the Baltic Fleet

Russian Imperial family aboard Standart. This is unattributed. Many hundreds of photographs of the Imperial family on board the Standart are available through the Beinecke Rare Book and Manuscript Library of Yale University, New Haven, CT.

Tsar's Russian Orthodox Chapel aboard Imperial Yacht Standart, 1896. Photographs commissioned by her Shipbuilders, Burmeister and Wain, Copenhagen, for her maiden voyage

sailors who had taken control of ships and bases now in defiance of the Provisional Government. Throughout the political 'dvoelastie' (February–October) *Standart* encouraged the formation of local soviets and herself hosted the Tsentrobalt aboard from April onwards.[4] Lenin's wife (Nadezhola Konstantinova Krupskaya) is even recorded on film aboard *Standart*, etching her name into the fabric with a ring, as Lenin tries to control and finally crush the revolt of the Kronstadt sailors in order to impose his own dictatorship.[5] In 1918 *Standart* took part in the legendary 'Ice Cruise', which saw the evacuation of Russian Baltic Fleet warships from Tallinn and Helsinki to Kronstadt with icebreakers to the fore, just in time to avoid capture by advancing German forces. Between 1935 and 1936 *Standart* was rebuilt as a fast minelayer, capable of deploying 320 mines and heavily armed with four 130 mm guns, seven 76.2 mm and three 45 mm anti-aircraft guns, among other armaments, and new engines. This made her one of the most advanced minelayers in

Russian Imperial Yacht Standart converted in the Second World War to fast minelayer in the Soviet Navy. Painting in Russian State Naval Archives (formerly the Central State Archives of the Navy of the Soviet Union) Painting unattributed.

the world, and she was dubbed uniquely a 'mine cruiser', receiving the Order of the Red Banner of the People's Commissariat of the Navy in 1938 for efficiency.[6] With so many former Imperial Navy officers absent from commands, the Soviet government decided to recall a number of these in the hope of new loyalties. *Standart's* Captain was one of these, Nikolai Iosifovich Meschersky, of princely descent. *Standart* was renamed *Vosemnadtsate Martza*, and subsequently *Marti*, and saw action minelaying on the first day of the war with the Soviet Union on 23 June 1941, and had to fight off U-boat attacks on 25 June, before reaching Tallinn.

She was damaged by the German Luftwaffe at Kronstadt Naval Base on 23 September 1941 but 'numerous gashes in the side of the ship' were repaired. She took part in the 240-mile voyage to relieve the defenders of Hango and on 3 April 1941 was awarded the rare title of one of the 'Guards' of the Homeland while in the midst of battle. She bombarded shore positions in the defence of Leningrad. She was renamed and served as training ship *Oka*

The last photograph of Empress Alexandra with Olga and Tatiana, Tobolsk 1918.

St Catherine's Chapel of St Peter and St Paul, St Petersberg Fortress where Tsar Nicholas, Alexandra and three daughters were re-interred in 2000.

through the Cold War until finally decommissioned and scrapped as late as 1961.

Two handwritten poems by the Holy Royal Martyr Grand Duchess Olga, were found at the Ipatiev House in Yekaterinburg, and appear in Sergei Bekhteyev's, *Songs of Russian Grief and Tears*.

There is the prayer entitled: 'Before the Icon of Our Lady':

> Of earth and heaven blessed Tsarina,
> Our only source of consolation,
> Lenient to every praying sinner.
> O, heed our humble supplication.
> Groping amid the dark of spite,
> Ensnared with evil's fiendish lace,
> We dare not complain at our plight,
> But give our Motherland Thy grace.
> The holy land of Russia, once blessed,
> Is now ordained to dire subversion,
> Of all the suffering Patroness,
> O save our country from incursion.
> Please, don't avert thine eyes from those
> Who thirst for Thy compassion,
> O, grant us hope for repose
> In our sorrow, and oppression.

Another is entitled, 'Prayer in Time of Trial and Tribulation':

> To Thee, Lord Gracious, we appeal:
> Help us to bear vilification
> And to share the ordeal.
> O Christ Redeemer, give us strength
> In ghastly woe never to repine,
> Help us surmount the bloodstained
> Way of the Cross with meek forbearance O' Thine.
> In days of outrageous tumult,
> O Lord Creator, give us power
> To bear injury and insult
> From looting enemies of ours.
> Almighty Lord, Benignant Master,
> Bless us with The divine orison,
> And in the hour of dire disaster
> Will give us peace Thy benison.
> And at the edge of doom impending

Rid us of fear and dismay
And grant us fortitude unending
For our Foes to humbly pray.

Tsarina Alexandra's Prayer, 1918

This prayer was found on the back of a postcard sent by the Empress to Alexsandr Syroboiarsky on 11 January 1918. The depiction on the postcard was of an Italian painting of Jesus wearing a crown of thorns, and gazing towards heaven. The prayer was written while the Tsarina and her family were under house arrest by the Bolsheviks in Tobolsk and suffering personal indignities, before their final removal to Ykaterinburg:

> O Lord, send us patience
> During these dark, tumultuous days
> To stand the people's persecution
> And the tortures of our executioners.
>
> Give us strength, O God so righteous
> To forgive our neighbour's wickedness
> And to greet the bloody, heavy cross
> With Your meekness.
>
> In these days of mutinous unrest
> When our enemies rob us,
> Christ the Saviour, help us
> Bear insult and disgrace.
>
> Lord of the world, God of the universe,
> Bless us with prayer
> And grant peace to the humble soul
> In this unbearable and fearful hour.
>
> And at the threshold of the grave
> Breathe a power that is beyond man
> Into the lips of Your slaves
> To pray meekly for their enemies.[7]

Prayers of a Romanian Princess

The Bolsheviks seized power during the Russian Revolution in October 1917, following Lenin's arrival in the 'sealed train' from Germany.

The true circumstances and route taken by this train between Zurich and the port of Sassnitz, opposite Malmo, before Lenin and his fellow 40 émigrés boarded a ship to cross the Baltic Sea to Sweden and onward travel by train to St Petersberg, still remain a mystery. In particular Michael Pearson has dwelt upon the unexplained stop of some 20 hours at Potsdam Station in Berlin, where he argues convincingly that Lenin received 40,000,000 gold marks from the German government, possibly even from the hands of Arthur Zimmerman himself, at a secret meeting (naturally denied by Lenin and Fritz Platten) at which Lenin also altered his entire plan for revolution from that first outlined during lunch at the Zaheringerhof in Zurich when the train began its journey.[8] Now there was to be no accommodation with a Socialist evolution from a peasant economy as determined by Marxist philosophy, but instead direct armed revolution and the imposition of Communism, by-passing the Socialist phase. Lenin had, in fact, while in Potsdam Station somehow suddenly conformed to the ideal progression advocated by Zimmerman and the German Kaiser to destabilize and topple the politicians in Russia who were prosecuting the war against Germany. Lenin was suddenly the recipient of massive resources that made possible what was inconceivable at the outset of the journey.

The upshot was soon felt across European monarchies. From the explanation given in December 1917 to the 7-year-old Princess Iliana in Jassy, Romania, by her mother that Father Christmas 'would not be able get over the German lines', the pawns on the military chessboard changed suddenly. Initially, the morale of the Russian troops declined further and the Romanian troops could not withstand the German advances as they occupied the country. But the Allies and Russia finally defeated Germany, though as a threat to their power the Tsar and his family were annihilated by the Bolsheviks in Russia. But this was only a brief respite for the Romanian monarchy as

Locomotive that pulled Lenin's train through Finland on the last leg of his 'sealed train' journey arriving on 3 April 1917 at Petrograd Station. The engine was donated by Finnish State Railways to the Soviet Union and is now preserved for display at Finlyandsky rail terminal, St Petersburg. Photograph by James G. Howes, 1998

the arrival of Russian troops in the Second World War brought exile at its conclusion.

Princess Iliana was held in much affection by the populace, not least for her extraordinary efforts in founding the Hospital of the Queen's Heart during the war where she nursed the war-wounded and diseased. She described at first hand the devastation of the German bombing raids, remarking of one incident at Bran that the approaching aeroplanes: 'were silver and beautiful against the blue sky, so that for an instant they seemed no part of war and destruction. Then suddenly the air was rent by a tremendous sound, and engulfing dust and acrid fumes seemed to surround us from all sides'. She led women and ran carrying a child to the

> dug out and jumped into a trench just as the second wave of bombs fell. When the dust had cleared a little for the second

time I found myself surrounded by weeping women and terrified girls. I was a little surprised to find that I felt no fear and that I could repeat the 91st Psalm. Slowly it calmed the others, and they quieted.[9]

But at the cessation of hostilities the Romanian Communist Party took power as a satellite of the Soviet Union, and Princess Iliana was refused permission to attend the seven-year memorial of her mother in Curtea de Arges. In grief she retreated to the chapel at Bran Castle where she had a revelation looking out at a mountain, concluding in her own words:

> So long had it stood there just like that – so very long: even before history began. It had been unchanged and unhurt by human strife and endeavour, by humiliations hopes and despairs. How small I and my pain were! And suddenly I understood that such things did not matter; that they were of no importance at all. Such things were there simply to be overcome; they were put in put way for us to use in the building of the staircase of life. On each one we could mount a step higher until finally we attain the Mountain. The eternal reality of living. I mention this because it was such a deep and real experience that it was one of the greatest events of my life.[10]

Iliana was destined for exile under the Communist government, who issued the ultimatum that the royal family could either leave Bucharest immediately or else choose to be confined to a monastery prior to execution. As she left the village of Tohan (whose occupants had originally donated an entire operating theatre to her hospital in days past and in return whose workers she treated free of charge for over four years) her car became stuck in mud. One of the villagers remarked 'see, the very earth is loath to let you go! But one request we still have of you. Will you kneel down with us and say a prayer for King and country, and for your return?' Iliana recorded that she did precisely that, 'joining in prayer with the factory workmen and those who till the soil. Our Father, Which art in heaven ...'.[11] This prayer was answered, for Iliana did eventually return to Romania over 40 years later.

In the meantime she founded a monastery in the American state of Pennsylvania on the basis that:

> we grew up with our faith, with the traditions and the habits of childhood. We carry it with us wherever we go ... The people in America's, their grandparents and great-grandparents came with the same traditions, but now, those are just folk tales they tell their children ... I can bring those traditions back and give them some of the peace that monasteries and the closeness to God have always given us.

Iliana (now Mother Alexandra) returned to Romania in 1990 following the fall of the Ceaucescu regime in 1989, to be greeted by 2,000 people at the railway station in Brasov, many of whom had been there when she left for exile in 1948.

The Chapel Royal possesses a magnificent magenta brocade stole made by Thomas Campbell of New York in 1984 from material commissioned by Mother Alexandra and used to make the set for officiating clergy at her monastery in Pennsylvania. The stole, now at St James's Palace, is therefore in close proximity to the remains of her grandmother's Orthodox chapel created within the Octagon Room of Clarence House. Much of the original paintwork of that chapel survives.

Greek Royal Family Prayers

God give him strength and patience.

(Princess of Wales, 1863)

This was the royal prayer of the Danish Alexandra, Princess of Wales (wife of the future King Edward VII of Great Britain and sister of King George I of Greece) to the Dowager Queen of Denmark in June 1863 a few days after Prince Christian William Ferdinand Adolphus George's acceptance of the Throne of Greece on 6 June as King George I of the Hellenes. He would succeed the deposed Otho, King of Greece. Ratification of his election as King George I by a treaty between the Protecting Powers and Denmark, following the appeal from the Hellenes submitted by the veteran Greek naval hero, Admiral Kanaris, took place on 13 July 1863. Four years later his sister, Dagmar

(Minny), was to marry the Tsarevich, the future Tsar Alexander II of Russia. This prayer and these relationships were to prove crucial to the survival of the Greek monarchy in years to come through war and peace.

Prince George I had wisely insisted that a condition of his taking the throne of Greece was that the Ionian Isles, including Corfu, would be ceded by Britain to Greece, thus currying genuine favour with the Greeks. Prince Philippos of Greece was to be rescued from this very island, the island of his birth, in December 1922, becoming in due course the husband of the future Queen Elizabeth II. But that was yet to come, and King George I of the Hellenes was determined to earn the acceptance of the Greek people. He began by refusing to make his First Communion according to the Lutheran Rites of Denmark, and instead made arrangements to be received into the Greek Orthodox Church as soon as he arrived in Athens. Before setting off for Greece King George I stayed with his sister at Marlborough House and paid a visit to Queen Victoria in October 1863. On his way to Balmoral he went first to the Greek Church in London Wall to attend a service. He was offered, but declined, a throne to sit upon, and stood instead according to Orthodox tradition, heard the 'Te Deum', and joined in unaccompanied hymns. Prayers offered by the chief Greek Orthodox priests also in Liverpool and Manchester included one for His Majesty, one for 'all the faithful', and another for those who had sacrificed their lives for Greek independence. George stopped over in Paris with the Emperor Napoleon arriving in Greece on 30 October 1863. In Greece King George's first official duty was to take the oath of fealty at the National Assembly on 31 October, during which he swore to protect 'in the name of the consubstantial and indivisible Trinity the dominant religion of the Greeks, to maintain and to defend the independence, the autonomy, and the integrity of the Greek state, and to observe its laws'[12]. King George turned out to be a most popular king, successfully weathering Balkan nationalism and Turkish defeat in the war of 1897, only to be assassinated in 1913.

His eldest son, Constantine, brother in law to the German

Kaiser, William II, succeeded him and tried his best to remain neutral during the First World War, but he was forced to abdicate in favour of his second son, Alexander, who in turn died from a monkey bite. Although Constantine was asked to return to the throne, the adverse consequences of war again with Turkey in 1922 led to his second abdication and in hair-raising escapes by various members of his family who were able to call upon their royal family ties across Europe to evade certain death. King Constantine issued a proclamation explaining that 'In order that my presence on the throne may not interfere with the sacred unity of the Hellenes and the assistance of our friends, and in order to avoid all misconception on the subject, I have abdicated'.[13]

King Constantine, Queen Sophie, Princesses Irene and Katherine, embarked just before midnight on 30 October 1922 on an old bug-infested steamer, SS *Patris*, bound for Palermo in Sicily. Meanwhile the elderly Queen Olga was staying at Sandringham as a guest of Queen Alexandra together with the Dowager Tsarina, and paid a visit to King George V at Windsor Castle. Her failing eyesight as she was kindly wheeled around in a bath chair occasioned her remarking upon catching sight of a bronze statue that it was evidently Queen Victoria. The attendant replied 'Oh no, Your Majesty, that is Lady Godiva!' King George V found this hilarious.[14] But anxiety was brewing over the fate of the Greek royal family as Prince Andrew was placed in solitary confinement and a collection of ministers and former prime ministers of Greece were shot by the revolutionaries. Queen Olga appealed for help to King George V, Alfonso XIII of Spain, and President Poincare of France. While representatives of the Pope and Alfonso arrived in Greece to plead for the life of Prince Andrew, King George V dispatched Captain Gerald Talbot, who successfully managed to persuade the revolutionary court to commute the death sentence instead to life in exile. The Prince was reunited with his wife and their five children on Corfu.

Sixth in succession to the Greek throne, Prince Philip had been born at 'Mon Repos' in Corfu and baptized at St George's Church at the Palaio Frouro (Old Fortress) in Haddokos. Queen

Olga and the entire town of Corfu, represented by a number of dignitaries, stood as godparents. Now 18 months later he and his family were rescued from Corfu by the HMS *Calypso*, a Royal Navy light cruiser,[15] in a top secret operation to pluck the Greek royal family from the shore.

Given that immediate action coupled with absolute secrecy was paramount to the success of this naval operation, there was literally no time to indulge in the niceties of the Foreign Office getting involved. Mindful of what had happened recently to the Romanovs in a period of revolution in Russia, King George V personally telephoned the Admiralty and requested a Royal Navy cruiser be detached from the Mediterranean Fleet to steam to Corfu and execute the rescue of the Greek royal family. This was accomplished under the command of Captain H.A. Buchanan Wollaston. And so the Foreign Office found itself after the event preparing a memorandum for Prime Minister Bonar Law to inform Parliament in due course. 'The original source of the instruction [The King] cannot be quoted. Perhaps the Prime Minister will be prepared to say that he instructed the Admiralty to issue the necessary orders.' Bonar Law appreciated the necessity to have acted with immediacy, and refused to distort the true explanation in any way. He therefore refused to comment and, thereby, avoided exposing the exiled royals to further danger until their future could be properly secured.

HMS *Calypso*, one of three 'War Emergency' 'Caledon' class cruisers (known as 'Tyrwhitt's Dreadnoughts'), was built by Hawthorne Leslie and launched on 21 June 1917. She had taken part in naval operations in the Baltic in November 1918 providing gunnery support to shore forces opposed to the Bolshevik revolutionaries – who were eventually to execute Prince Philip's Russian relations. Along with her sister ship HMS *Caradoc*, and three destroyers (*Vendetta*, *Vortigern* and *Wakeful*), she captured the Bolshevik destroyers, *Avtroil* and *Spartak* off Reval. She also took part in the Second Battle of Heligoland Bight in which an 11-inch shell destroyed her bridge, killing all the bridge crew and the Captain.

Now off Corfu, the Greek royal family boarded with an absolute minimum of possessions, Prince Philip being carried in

HMS Calypso

an adapted orange box. HMS *Calypso* sailed to Brindisi, where the family was put on board a train destined for Paris. One account details that Prince Philip was eager to explore as much of the train as he could on the journey, and arriving at Paris they were housed by Prince Philip's Aunt – Princess Marie Bonaparte. The second son of King George I and Queen Olga of Greece, another George, had contracted a civil marriage on 21 November 1907 (and later a religious marriage on 12 December 1907 in Athens) to Marie Bonaparte. She was the daughter of Roland Bonaparte, Grandson of Lucien Bonaparte who was Emperor Napoleon Bonaparte I's brother. Roland was a great scientist, President of the Societe de Geographie from 1910, after whom 'Napoleon Point' in Antarctica was named by Jean-Baptiste Charcot.

In the Second World War HMS *Calypso* went on to serve with the 7th Cruiser Squadron in North Atlantic waters between Scotland and Iceland, and took part in the hunt for the *Scharnhorst* and *Gneisenau* following the sinking of the *Rawalpindi*. In 1940 she was redeployed to the eastern Mediterranean when on 12 June, two days after Italy declared war on Great Britain, she was sunk by a torpedo fired from the Italian Submarine, *Bagnolini,* captained by C.C. Franco Tosoni Pittoni,

50 miles off Cape Lithion, Crete, while on patrol preventing shipping reaching Libya. Thirty-nine crew died and the survivors were rescued by HMS *Dainty* and taken to Alexandria.

Just six months later, in January 1941, Prince Philip, by then serving in the Royal Navy on HMS *Ramilles* off Ceylon escorting troopships bound from Australia to Egypt, was transferred to the battleship HMS *Valiant*, stationed in Alexandria, aboard which Prince Philip served as searchlight controller in the sinking of two Italian cruisers at the Battle of Matapan on 28–29th March 1941. Prince Philip was later in North Atlantic convoy duties, and returned to the Mediterranean in July 1943 for 'Operation Husky' (the invasion of Sicily) aboard HMS *Wallace*, and at the close of the war was present aboard HMS *Whelp* at the Japanese surrender in Tokyo Bay.

By Royal Warrant 'Philip, Duke of Edinburgh' is singled out by name and title in State Prayers in the Book of Common Prayer, immediately after the 'Prayer for The Queen's Majesty'.

Notes

[1] Quoted in S. Mironenko and A. Maylunas, *A Life Long Passion. Nicholas and Alexandra Their Own Story* (New York: Doubleday, 1997), p. 352.

[2] A photograph exists of this Orthodox chapel and is displayed at Tsar Alexander's Palace. A detailed description of the vessel is found in Alexander M. Golubev and Andrei L. Larionev, *Maria Feodorovna, Empress of Russia. An Exhibition about the Danish Princess who became Empress of Russia* (Copenhagen Palace Exhibition Fund, 1997), pp. 230–6.

[3] Beken of Cowes possesses a series of photographs of *Standart* in the Solent, and the Imperial War Museum of the *Poliarnaia Zvesda*. *Janes Fighting Ships of World War II* contains images of both vessels.

[4] P.E. Dybenko, *Die Rebellen, Erinnerungen aus der* Revolution, Vienna-Berlin, Vlg.f.Lit u Pol, 1932. These are the memoirs of Bolshevik sailors' leaders, especially Tsentrebalt chairmanships hosted aboard *Standart* in 1917.

[5] Contemporary film clips of 1917–18 assembled as *The Russian Revolution in Colour*, ABC TV Channel, 5 and 12 January 2008.

[6] M.E. Malevinskaya, *Rossiiskii gosudarstvennyi arkhiv VMF. Spravochnik pofondam (1917–1940)* (Sankt-Peterburg: Blits, 1995). These two

volumes describe the holdings of the Russian State Naval Archives in St Petersburg for the years 1917 until 1940. Part I comprises 11 sections beginning with the Provisional Government, and includes Tsentrobalt affairs and other fleet matters including indexes to ships and events.

7   M.D. Steinberg and V.L. Krustalev, *The Fall of the Romanovs*, and Russian documents translated by E. Tucker (New Haven, CT, and London: Yale University Press, 1995), p. 221.

8   M. Pearson, *The Sealed Train* (New York: Putnam, 1975), ch. 7 'Berlin and the Big Idea'.

9   HRH Ileana, Princess of Romania, *I Live Again* (New York: Rinehart, 1952).

10 HRH Ileana, Princess of Romania, *I Live Again* (New York: Rinehart, 1952).

11 HRH Ileana, Princess of Romania, *I Live Again* (New York: Rinehart, 1952).

12 *The Times*, 18 November 1863.

13 *Illustrated London News*, 7 October 1922.

14 Nicholas, Prince of Greece, *My Fifty Years* (London: Hutchinson, 1926), pp. 315–16.

15 *Jane's Fighting Ships of World War I* (Coulsdon: Janes's Publishing Company, 1919).

11

Royal Prayers of Dedication to Right Governance in Nation, Empire and Commonwealth

A Prayer for Indian Princes, for Use during the Royal Visit to India, November 1911

We make our prayer to Thee, O merciful God, for all Indian Princes and Rulers within the Empire, beseeching Thee so to guide and bless them, that under them Thy people may lead peaceable lives in all godliness and honesty; through Jesus Christ our Lord. Amen.

The Earl of Meath's Prayer for Empire Governance

O God, Who hast made us members of the British Empire, and hast bound us together by one King and one Flag, may we ever live in remembrance of our great responsibilities, and be mindful that 'righteousness exalteth a nation'. Help us to seek to excel in the practice of faith, courage, duty self-discipline, fair dealing, even justice, and true sympathy, that, as loyal patriots and good citizens, we may each individually aid in elevating the British character, and as a God-fearing and God-loving people glorify Thee, the King of kings and Lord of lords; through Jesus Christ Thy Son. Amen.

Coronation Prayer of 1936

This was composed by the Bishop of Norwich, 'for use throughout the Empire and at the Queen's Hall 'Coronation Day of Intercession and Conference' on 11 May 1936. It is lengthy, covering the death of King George V and alluding to the subsequent Abdication of King Edward VIII in the words:

O God, Who in mysterious ways dost perform Thy wonders among men, we praise Thee for the King whom Thou has given to us to sit upon the Throne of Thy faithful servant, his father, and through Thy favour to carry forward at home and abroad the works and ways of him whose name he bears; in humble gratitude we acknowledge Thee the spirit in which he accepted the heavy task that Thou has entrusted to him, for his courage, and industry which steadied the nation in time of shock and strain...the claims of Caesar and the claims of God are not conflicting: our loyalty is pledged to a Christian Prince and Ruler. In rendering to him the things which are his, we are accomplishing a part of our duty of rendering to God the things which are God's. 'By Me kings reign, and princes decree justice.'

Queen Elizabeth's Declaration of Sovereignty, 1952

Princess Elizabeth was still in Africa when the tragic news of her father's death reached the royal party in 1952, and so the first part of the Accession Council was held in the Picture Gallery of the State Apartments in St James's Palace on the day of King George VI's death on 6 February 1952. The second part of the Accession Council could not convene until 8 February at 10 a.m., the morning after The Queen's return from Africa, she having spent the night in the adjoining Clarence House. A total of 175 Privy Counsellors gathered in the Entrée Room of the State Apartments, adjacent to Throne Room, where a leading delegation of them were then ushered by the Lord Chamberlain, the Earl of Clarendon, to be received by The Queen in private. She then entered the Entrée Room and addressed the entire company with her Declaration of Sovereignty, including her royal prayer, saying:

Your Royal Highnesses, My Lords, Ladies and Gentlemen: On the sudden death of my dear father I am called to fulfil the duties and responsibilities of Sovereignty. At this time of deep sorrow it is a profound consolation to me to be assured of the sympathy which you and all my people feel towards me, to my mother, and my sister, and to the other members of my family. My father was our revered and beloved head as he was of the

12

Royal Prayers of Royal Patronage

Bestowal of royal patronage has always been of great benefit to numerous charitable endeavours in aid of the disadvantaged, as well as to other national assets such as wards and hospitals, where lacunae have been observed in the workings of state provision. Initiatives promoted by royals can be enormously effectual, as with Queen Victoria's 'Indian Famine Fund' in 1897. This raised a staggering £2 million, a figure which, when translated into modern currency, far exceeded the impressive British efforts to raise funds for famine relief in Africa in the mid-1980s.

Royal patronage and the prayers that go with it, have never been a field taken unadvisedly by the royal family. There is a delicate path to tread. King George III firmly believed that poor children throughout the Dominions should be able to read the Bible, but this was thought even by some church factions to be dangerous 'levelling'. High Churchmen viewed non-conformist and evangelical elements of the Christian church with suspicion and no little alarm. When the champion of education for the poor, Joseph Lancaster, turned up to seek an audience with King George III at Windsor, the Dean told him to clear off and mind his own business. But, undaunted, he succeeded in obtaining an audience with the King, who turned out to be a great supporter of his endeavours. The King lent his support to the Lancastrian schools but cautioned him not to 'tease' the local Anglicans in Windsor. The effect of this support was to galvanize the Anglicans into action in the same field to claw back some of the King's favour. Thus was born in 1811 'The National Society for Promoting the Education of the Poor in the Principles of the Established Church Schools'. This was quickly granted royal patronage and a balanced royal portfolio cleverly restored by means of grants of thousands of pounds from the royal family, including the Prince Regent (previously a strong supporter of Lancaster), and the Dukes of York, Cumberland and Cambridge.

Applying adroit diplomacy the King and the Dukes of Kent and Sussex (the latter two supporters of Dissenter endeavours) maintained their close association with the British and Foreign School Society (BFSS). By 1820 the National Society and the BFSS had between them over 145,000 pupils in school – and were to provide the base for the later government initiatives in education. Although the royal family has steered away from political factions and parties, they have not been frightened off supporting an obviously good cause merely because of its political unpopularity. Edward Augustus, Duke of Kent (1767–1820) once remarked 'true charity is of no particular party, but is the cause of all parties',[1] thereby retaining the justification for royal support of causes abandoned by state politics.

In her 1832 tour of the industrial heartlands of England at the initiative of her mother, the Duchess of Kent, in which she was appalled by the wretched conditions of the coal-mining districts with their blackened huts and the poorly clothed children, combined with visits to Chester and Shrewsbury, Princess Victoria saw some of the realities of daily life. The Duchess of Kent resolved in her reply of thanks to the welcome they received from the bishop and clergy in Chester Cathedral to encourage the Princess to act on her observations: 'I cannot allude to your good feelings towards the Princess, than by joining fervently in the wish, that she may set an example in her conduct of that piety towards God, and charity towards man, which is the only sure foundation either of individual happiness or national prosperity.'[2] And so in 1833 Princess Victoria accepted her first patronage. In just three years she accepted: Infant Orphan Asylum, the Children's Friend Society and the London Ophthalmic Hospital, Moorfields. Others followed and many have become household names today, such as her royal patronage of the Society for the Prevention of Cruelty to Animals, which before her royal patronage, granted in 1840, was literally on its last legs and 'relieved its supporters from all anxiety about its future'.

This, 1840, was the year of Queen Victoria's wedding to Prince Albert in the Chapel Royal at St James's Palace and in honour of that the Bristol Royal Infirmary named two new wards 'Victoria' and 'Albert', and in 1850 it attracted royal patronage to become the 'Bristol Royal Infirmary'. But Bristol was a divided city politically with its hospitals attracting the support of the Liberals, who did not wish to apply for royal patronage, and the infirmary, supported by Tories, who did. This led to the quip that 'The patient who wants a sovereign remedy will now go to the royal infirmary; but those who want a radical cure will go to the Hospital'.

Other hospitals were similarly chequered with political adherence: in London Bart's was Tory, St Thomas's was Whig. But support of hospitals and plight of the sick outweighed the politics and ultimately this was a blessing, for it was royal support that saved the voluntary London hospitals from whole-sale closure in post-First World War years due to the success of the '1922 Save Your Hospitals Appeal!' and formed an unlikely bridge to the expansion of what was to become state hospital provision with the creation in 1919 of the Ministry of Health and the Dawson Report of 1920. The next 40 years were to see the rise of the welfare state as an experiment conducted in the face of the royal family, with the Lambeth Conference Resolution of 1948 even seeing the Church seduced with the notion that social engineering from government could bring about the New Jerusalem and should be embraced in their decision that:

the State is under the moral law of God, and is intended by Him to be an instrument for human welfare. We therefore welcome the growing concern and care of the modern State for its citizens, and call upon the Church members to accept their own political responsibility and to co-operate with the State and its officers in their work.

This policy immediately placed the Church's time-honoured and traditional initiatives at the behest of the central apparatus of the state and membership of the Church began its dramatic decline. It was a shot in the foot, but not a mistake made by the monarchy. They knew from thousands of years of experience that it was individuals who changed the world for the better, largely irrespective, and often in response to the failings, of the prevailing political system of the moment.

The Duke of Edinburgh in 'A Question of Balance' has concluded that the greatest weakness of Marxist historical imperialism

> is that it ignores the purely voluntary and altruistic elements in human nature which are encouraged to flourish in any civilized human society. The concept of charity (in the voluntary sense), or of obligation, or of social conscience, hardly exists in Marxist doctrine but there are vast numbers of people of all classes in this country who give money generously to charities and who give their leisure time and energies to voluntary organizations of all kinds and who respond with astonishing speed to the needs of the victims of natural and man-made disasters all over the world. This cannot be swept aside as a sort of fringe phenomenon peculiar to the bourgeoisie and unworthy of consideration by serious political and economic commentators. It is a vitally important factor in life and the very best example of individual initiative and sense of responsibility.[3]

The number of royal patronages, and their sheer spread across the daily lives of the citizenry of the UK bears this out. The voluntary sector is very much the monarch's domain and there is a realization from government that without the voluntary sector the nation's welfare would decline. The monarchy has a special bond with the youth and they are alike in that they renew themselves generationally – they grow old together and produce the next generation together. This is not an option for political ideologists. And so, King George V found himself in his Empire speech of 1935 advocating support for the Prince of Wales's Commemorative Fund. This was to become the King George V Jubilee Trust – forerunner of the 1976 Prince's Trust that has proved so overwhelmingly beneficial to the disadvantaged in their efforts to better their conditions and to realize commercial potential. Government authorities have belatedly come to seek royal advice as to how such things are achieved. The Prince of Wales through his Patronage of the Prince's Initiative for Mature Enterprise (PRIME) has established the only national organization dedicated to helping people aged over 50 set up in business. In 2005–06 the Prince helped to raise a whopping £110 million to support the work of his own 16 core charities.

Royal prayer in the patronage sector is two way. Prayers for the work and example of royal patrons in the field of health and welfare, for example, are represented in such invocations as are to be found within the workings of 'The Royal Sailors Rest' (Aggies).

Following Miss Agnes Weston's achievements in establishing Rests for fellowship and Christian reflection among army personnel stationed in Bath in the 1860s and at Plymouth from 1873, her association with Portsmouth, even today in the minds of many sailors, came as a result of a national tragedy in 1878 – the loss of the frigate HMS *Euridyce* with most of her crew of 320. Agnes immediately went to Portsmouth to try to see what suffering she could relieve and made a nationwide tour to raise money, both for the Rest and for the bereaved. She worked tirelessly for naval wives and families, and was instrumental in getting widows pensions introduced in 1894.

The Royal Warrant bestowing 'Royal' on the Sailors Rests was awarded after the Royal Naval Exhibition at the Chelsea Hospital in 1892. In 1898 Agnes was summoned to Windsor to meet the Queen and in 1901 she received an honorary degree from Glasgow University, among the first ever awarded to a woman.

Agnes died in 1918, aged 78, and was buried with full naval honours, the first time such an honour had been given to a woman. Her gravestone gives her name, dates and the simple epitaph: 'The Sailor's Friend'

The following prayers are offered from 'RSR Prayer Support – Summer 2008':

Light of the world
When Jesus spoke again to the people, he said, 'I am the light of the world. Whoever follows me will never walk in darkness, but will have the light of life'. John 8.12

Please pray for ...
The Naval, Military and Air Force Bible Society as they seek to bring the Word of the Lord to all.

The Naval Christian Fellowship, its network of contacts worldwide and the support and encouragement they give to service personnel.

All those serving in HM Forces, that wherever they are they will experience God's care and guidance. May they encounter God through the love and friendship of the Christian community.

All in our nation who do not know the love of Jesus, that they will turn to Christ and that once more His banner will be lifted high throughout the land. Give thanks that we are able to worship freely and for the peace and security we enjoy in this country.
Prayer days to be continued:
Days 23 to 26:

Pure joy:
Consider it pure joy, my brothers, whenever you face trials of many kinds, because you know that the testing of your faith develops perseverance. James 1: 2-3

Please pray for ...
RSR's Patron Her Majesty the Queen: Give thanks for her Christian faith, and pray that it be a powerful witness throughout this nation and to the wider world.

Extracts from a Speech Delivered by HRH The Prince of Wales to the Prayer Book Society's Annual Conference, Oxford, 14 September 2006

It does seem to me that one of the great tragedies of our modern existence is that all the signposts, all those marvellous 'little country lanes' that people used to know and walk down, have all been destroyed, so that there are so few things that anybody can share with their grandparents if you are younger, which I think is a real and tragic loss. How you knit back again some of these lost aspects of life, how you join the roots again which have been severed, is something, for what it's worth, that I've been trying to do for the past thirty years.

It does gives me enormous pleasure as your Patron to join you at your Annual Conference. It is particularly appropriate that you have chosen to meet in Oxford to commemorate the 450th anniversary of the martyrdom in this city of Archbishop Thomas Cranmer ...

... Then after being selected as a junior member of an embassy to Spain in 1527, he had his first fateful meeting with King Henry VIII and the quiet academic became a leading actor in the affairs which preoccupied the whole of Europe.

So I think this anniversary is a marvellous opportunity to tell Cranmer's story and the story of The Book of Common Prayer, if we possibly can, to a new generation ...

... It is sometimes forgotten that the Prayer Book largely created and spread standard English across the country in the 16th century, as a result of Sunday worship in the parish church when, week after week, millions would assemble to hear the power and majesty of the Book of Common Prayer ...

... It also needs to be remembered, I think, that standard English could have developed in other ways. For example, the pompous and convoluted style favoured by some humanist scholars with an excessive dependence on the classical languages, or the path favoured by men like Sir John Cheke, Cranmer's friend, which would have seen a consistent preference for Anglo-Saxon derivations over Latin and Greek. He proposed, for instance, that instead of 'resurrection' we should speak of 'gainrising'; 'crucified' would have been 'crossed' and proselyte, 'freshman'.

And the influence of the Prayer Book upon many generations has, I believe, gone beyond its language and has played a major role in instilling in English culture the essential virtues of restraint and balance. It has reminded us – but perhaps not enough – that if we encourage the use of mean, trite and ordinary language, we encourage a mean, trite and ordinary view of the world we inhabit.

The genius of Cranmer's Prayer Book – in my humble opinion – lies in the conveyance of a sense of the sacred through the power and majesty of the language so that, in the words of the Collect 'Among the sundry and manifold changes of the world, our hearts may surely there be fixed where true joys are to be found'.

The Prayer Book also offers a simple and moderate system for a whole life, from baptism to last rites, and seeks, I think, in its rubrics and ceremonies to embrace the whole person and not merely the intellect.

It is for these reasons that I congratulate the Prayer Book Society for all its work in fostering the traditions of the Prayer Book and for telling its story as a system which transforms lives and translates doctrines and ethics into a living ethos ...

While the Prince of Wales is Patron of the Prayer Book Society he has embraced the right of other faiths to contribute their understanding to the workings of the society in which we live. In an essay he contributed on 'The Alliance of Civilizations and Interfaith Reconciliation', published by the University of Maryland in 2006, the Prince of Wales remarked that:

I know only too well how one's faith can be challenged, having lost a much-loved great uncle, Lord Mountbatten, in an IRA terrorist bomb attack in 1979. But I remember how it gradually dawned on me that thoughts of vengeance and hatred would merely prolong the terrible law of cause and effect and continue an unbroken cycle of violence. 'An eye for an eye', said Mahatma Gandhi, 'and soon the whole world is blind.' I have also come to see that the universal truths of the great religions do teach us something of the unfathomable mysteries of our existence and how to cope not only with human free will but also with the giant paradoxes of life itself ... The Torah, the Gospels, the Quran all testify to the same truth and the religions of India also see the divine spirit in creation.[4]

The Prince of Wales reminds us that:

The word religion means re-establishing the bond (the Latin origin of the word re-legio), the ligament between Man and God that Man lost at the Fall. Every religion is thus like a rope thrown down from Heaven for fallen Man to cling to, and that rope is an aspect of the Divine Word. Each of the religions recognizes that all is not right with the world.[5]

Notes

[1] Quoted in F. Prochaska, *Royal Bounty: The Making of a Welfare Monarchy* (London: Yale University Press, 1995), p. 36.

[2] Quoted in G.N. Wright, *The Life and Reign of William the Fourth*, vol. 2, 1837, p. 756.

[3] HRH The Duke of Edinburgh, *A Question of Balance* (London: Michael Russell, 1982), pp. 24–5.

[4] HRH The Prince of Wales, *Religion – The Ties that Bind, A Series of essays on The Alliance of Civilizations and Interfaith Reconciliation*, eds S. Bushrui and D. Cadman (College Park, MD: University of Maryland, 2006), p. 3.

[5] HRH The Prince of Wales *Religion – The Ties that Bind, A Series of essays on The Alliance of Civilizations and Interfaith Reconciliation*, eds S. Bushrui and D. Cadman (College Park, MD: University of Maryland, 2006), p. 5.

13

Royal Remembrance – Silent Royal Prayer

For rulers are not a terror to good works, but to the evil. Wilt thou then not be afraid of the power? Do that which is good, and thou shalt have praise of the same: for he is the minister of God to thee for good. But if thou do that which is evil, be afraid; for he beareth not the sword in vain; for he is the minister of God, a revenger to execute wrath upon him that doeth evil. Wherefore ye must needs be subject, not only for wrath, but also for conscience sake. For this cause pay ye tribute also; for they are God's ministers, attending continually upon this very thing. Render therefore to all their dues; tribute to whom tribute is due, custom to whom custom, fear to whom fear, honour to whom honour. (St Paul's epistle to the Romans 13.3-7, now employed as the Epistle for the Fourth Sunday after The Epiphany in the 1662 Book of Common Prayer)

In the matter of national remembrance, the Sovereign has struck a balance between the need for a Christian justification for the loss of so much life in the pursuit of a just war, and the equally important need to remember the sacrifice made by those of different, or no, belief who died as comrades in the same ethical cause of freedom and justice. Royal prayer has tended to be a private and unspoken element out there on parade grounds and cemeteries during ceremonials of remembrance. At the same time, the physical presence of the Sovereign and members of the royal family, whose responsibilities heading various units of the armed forces are symbolized in the uniforms they wear upon such occasions, also represents those of other faiths (and none) whose sacrifice for this, and allied countries, in the same cause is thus equally remembered.

Silence as Prayer

King George V ordered the now familiar two minutes' silence for Remembrance ceremonies in response to a paper submitted to him by Lord Milner from the War Cabinet on 5 November 1919. The origin of the idea of a period of silence to remember the fallen, as well as those on active service far from home, lay in South Africa during the Great War. The son of former High Commissioner to the Dominion of South Africa, Sir Percy Fitzpatrick, was killed in France in 1917. On 4 November 1919 Sir Percy drafted a minute for the consideration of the War Cabinet, writing:

> In the hearts of our people there is a real desire to find some lasting expression of their feeling for those who gave their lives in the war. They want something done now while the memories of sacrifice are in the minds of all; for there is the dread – too well grounded in experience – that those who have gone will not always be first in the thoughts of all, and that when the fruits of their sacrifice become our daily bread, there will be few occasions to remind us of what we realise so clearly today.
>
> During the War, we in South Africa observed what we called the 'Three minutes' pause'. At noon each day, all work, all talk and all movement were suspended for three minutes that we might concentrate as one in thinking of those – the living and the dead – who had pledged and given themselves for all that we believe in …
>
> Silence, complete and arresting, closed upon the city – the moving, awe inspiring silence of a great Cathedral where the smallest sound must seem a sacrilege … Only those who have felt it can understand the overmastering effect in action and reaction of a multitude moved suddenly to one thought and one purpose.[1]

Sir Percy's proposal was aired in Cabinet on 5 November 1919, which approved a 'Service of Silence' on Armistice Day, but determined that the duration of silence be one minute and not three minutes, subject to the approval of the King. This was based upon the precedent of a one minute silence observed at Theodore Roosevelt's funeral following his death on the 6 January earlier in the year.

Roosevelt's son Archie had observed that 'the old lion is dead', while Thomas Marshall, Vice-President, alluding to his support for so many worthy causes, remarked, 'Death had to take Roosevelt sleeping, for if he had been awake, there would have been a fight'. As it happens Roosevelt was a Presbyterian and Freemason who believed firmly in the separation of Church from State, and objected to the Deity being mentioned on common American currency in the motto 'In God we trust'.

Lord Milner drafted a 'personal request' to the King and took it to Buckingham Palace. King George V discussed it with his Lord Stamfordham, his Private Secretary, and altered the duration of the silence to two minutes. Milner then reported back to Cabinet and prepared a final draft as agreed by the King for release to the Dominions and the press. This was carried by all national newspapers on 7 November 1919 as a common text:

> Tuesday next, November 11, is the first anniversary of the Armistice, which stayed the world wide carnage of the four preceding years and marked the victory of Right and Freedom. I believe that my people in every part of the Empire fervently wish to perpetuate the memory of the Great Deliverance, and of those who have laid down their lives to achieve it. To afford an opportunity for the universal expression of this feeling, it is my desire and hope that at the hour when the Armistice came into force, the eleventh hour of the eleventh day of the eleventh month, there may be for the brief space of two minutes a complete suspension of our normal activities. No elaborate organisation appears to be required. At a given signal, which can easily be arranged to suit the circumstances of the locality, I believe that we shall gladly interrupt our business and pleasure, whatever it may be and unite in this simple service of Silence and Remembrance.

The King's 'simple service of Silence and Remembrance' was observed throughout the Realm and Empire. The observations of one local newspaper were common to many as the *Western Morning News and Mercury* issue of 12 November 1919 recorded:

> For two minutes after the hour of eleven had struck yesterday

morning Plymouth stood inanimate with the nation ... Two minutes before the hour the maroons boomed out their warning in one long drawn out note ... As the hour struck a great silence swept over the town. People halted in their walks, chatter ceased as if by magic, traffic stopped and the rumbling note of industry stayed.

The Cenotaph

It was particularly important, following the conclusion of the Great War, that any other international symbol of remembrance be non-denominational. The British War Cabinet needed to have a way of permitting thousands to remember fallen comrades in the course of the forthcoming celebration to mark the Peace Treaty of 28 June 1919, and formed a Peace Celebrations Committee, chaired by Lord Curzon. Its first meeting took place on 9 May 1919 and a decision was made to mount a victory parade, but incorporating the opportunity to salute the dead. Sir Alfred Mond as First Commissioner of the Board of Works recommended Sir Edwin Lutyens as a suitable architect to design an appropriate temporary monument that could serve the purpose in Whitehall on the route of the parade, which was also to pass Buckingham Palace. The Imperial War Museum possesses a design by Lutyens for a Cenotaph, dated 4 June 1919. But what swung the issue in the direction of the design now held in such respect and affection in Whitehall was the initiative of Sir Lionel Earle, Permanent Secretary of the Office of Works, whose letter of 13 May 1919 to the Earl of Danby, British Ambassador to France, elicited in his response details of the remembrance element of the parade the French were intending to hold in Paris on 14 July 1919. Minutes of the British Peace Celebrations Committee held on 18 June 1919[2] reveal that President Clemenceau had confided in Lloyd George that the French were going to parade past a 'great catafalque' to be erected temporarily next to the Arc de Triomphe, and which the troops would salute as they marched past in honour of their fallen comrades. Lloyd George attended this ceremony and was deeply moved. He returned even more determined to see the creation of a point of homage for Britain and its Empire in mourning for its million dead.

In early July Sir Edwin Lutyens had been invited to Downing Street and tasked with designing and constructing a suitable monument in two weeks. Immediately after meeting the Prime Minister he met Sir Frank Baines, Chief Architect of the Office of Works, and there and then sketched for him a design and followed this up with a wooden model, now also preserved in the Imperial War Museum. The upshot was a wooden and plaster structure which was unveiled on 19 July 1919, past which 1,500 officers and 15,000 other ranks from many allied nations marched in silence, led by Allied Commanders, and all saluted as they passed by. The King reviewed the parade from a pavilion erected temporarily outside Buckingham Palace. The structure and ceremonial caught the public's mood and need to grieve, and a letter to *The Times* from 'R.I.P.' observed: 'The new Cenotaph in Whitehall is so simple and dignified that it would be a pity to consider it merely as a temporary structure.'

It was Captain Ormsby-Gore who raised in the House of Commons the question of replacing the temporary cenotaph with a permanent one in Whitehall. At the same time he and 23 other MPs signed a petition to Sir Alfred Mond requesting the permanent structure. Lutyens recalled:

> Time passed and the plain fact emerged and grew stronger every hour that the Cenotaph was what the people wanted, and that they wanted to have the wood and plaster original replaced by an identical memorial in lasting stone. It was a mass-feeling too deep to express itself more fitly than by piles of fresh flowers which loving hands placed on the Cenotaph day by day. Thus it was decided, by the human sentiment of millions, that the Cenotaph should be as it is now, and speaking as the designer, I would wish for no greater honour, no more complete and lasting satisfaction.

Upon being told by Sir Alfred Mond that 'Unless it were removed within the next nine or ten days it would probably crumble to pieces' the Cabinet decided upon a permanent structure, but favouring a site in The Mall. This was overturned in discussion, it being realized that so many memories already surrounded the site in Whitehall. Yet Westminster City Council, whose duty it was to grant or withhold planning permission, favoured a site in Parliament Square. Mond took legal council from the Treasury Solicitors as to whether the Board of Works might proceed without Council permission but erred on the side of caution; instead writing thus to the Mayor:

> Before the Council come to a final decision on this question I should like them to bear in mind that the erection of the permanent Memorial is the declared decision of the Cabinet supported by the House of Commons and public opinion. With regard to the Committee's suggestion that the Cenotaph should be erected in Parliament Square or elsewhere, I think it should be remembered that it was specially designed by Sir Edwin Lutyens for the position in which it stands and with the most careful regard for its surroundings. The spot on which it stands is now consecrated to the Memory of all those, whether belonging to the Empire or our Allies, who fell in the Great War, and it will thus be remembered for all time the spot containing the Memorial to the 'Glorious Dead' which was saluted by the representatives of the troops of the Empire and of our Allies on the day when Peace in the Greatest War in the World's history was celebrated in London.

The question was finally settled at a meeting of Westminster County Council with the motion that Parliament Square was more suitable being defeated, and the permanent Cenotaph in Whitehall eventually left as the favoured option.

The stone quarried for the Whitehall Cenotaph was taken from the north side of Perryfield Quarries on Portland Bill in the angle of the railway cuttings opposite the Mermaid Inn and Portland Museum at the Pennsylvania Castle end of Wakeham's Street, under two fields called 'Pitt's Ground' and 'Above Coombe'. The operation was executed by Holland, Hannen and Cubitts Limited at a cost of £7,325, Lutyens waiving his fee. The cost was met by funds voted through Parliament. Yet quarrying and shipping stone from Portland Bill was not always so easily accomplished. Upon William of Orange's successful invasion in 1688, Christopher Wren found that enlarging

Kensington Palace for the new king and queen, together with other building endeavours, was often subject to interference from French warships that deliberately set out to blockade Portland Bill. Such was the disruption caused that Queen Mary sent a letter to King William in Ireland with a report that building works had again stopped owing to a French blockade of Portland.

The Cenotaph itself incorporates the smallest stone joints rubbed since the Parthenon was built in the 5th century bc. Although Lutyens did not visit Athens until 1932, he applied the ancient Greek method of entasis so as to avoid a single vertical or horizontal line The 'verticals' if extended would converge at a point over 1,000 feet above the ground, while the 'horizontals', being radials of a circle, find their centre at 900 feet below ground. The Cenotaph deliberately omits any religious symbol, because it commemorates those of all creeds and none.

King George V unveiled the stone Cenotaph on 11 November 1920, as part of the ceremonial marking the passing of the Unknown Warrior for re-burial at Westminster Abbey. The first annual ceremony began in 1921. But with the world at war again, Lutyens left word before he died in 1944 that the cenotaph should once more honour the dead of a world war but that nothing should be added by way of decoration, other than the inscribing of the dates of the Second World War at its conclusion. At the conclusion of hostilities he was supported by the founder of the Imperial War Graves Commission, General Sir Fabian Ware, who replied to a letter from Admiral of the Fleet Lord Chatfield:

> My personal view is that new dates only should be added to the Cenotaph, and I should deprecate any competing monument or any structural addition to the Cenotaph (which would be aesthetically unpardonable). At the same time, it seems to me almost impossible to pick out a beneficent object which would command universal assent.[3]

And so at the commencement of the remembrance ceremony on 10 November 1946, King George VI unveiled the dates MCMXXXIX (1939) and MCMXLV (1945) which had been inscribed on the upper portions of the east and west faces by John Lake, Chief Monumental Mason to The Crown, who had himself been responsible for depositing statues of national importance down Welsh Coal Mines for protection, and was later to take office as a vestryman with the Chapel Royal.

Silent Royal Prayer in Flanders Fields

In Flanders fields the poppies blow
Between the crosses, row on row,
That mark our place; and in the sky The larks,
still bravely singing, fly
Scarce heard amid the guns below.

We are the Dead. Short days ago
We lived, felt dawn, saw sunset glow,
Loved and were loved, and now we lie
In Flanders fields.

Take up our quarrel with the foe:
To you from failing hands we throw
The torch; be yours to hold it high.
If ye break faith with us who die
We shall not sleep,
Though poppies grow
In Flanders fields.

Canadian military doctor, John McCrae, began writing this poem on the same evening as the death of his friend, Lieutenant Alexis Helmer, who was killed by a German artillery shell on 2 May 1915 during the Second Battle of Ypres. McCrea himself died in a military hospital on the northern French coast shortly after writing his poem. But it made it to publication, and reading it in *Punch Magazine* an American War Secretary, Moina Michael, began to sell poppies to raise funds for ex-Service personnel, and from this came the red poppy as a symbol of remembrance for the fallen and the Legion Poppy Day, first held in Britain on 11 November 1921. In 1922 Major George Howson realized that ex-servicemen could perhaps make artificial poppies and approached the British Legion in 1922, ending up founding a

small factory that was to become the Royal British Legion Poppy
Factory.

King George V was so moved upon visiting the First World
War battlefields of Flanders in 1922 that he issued the statement:
'We can truly say that the whole circuit of the earth is girdled
with the graves of our dead ... I have many times asked myself
whether there can be more potent advocates of peace upon earth
... than this massed multitude of silent witnesses to the
desolation of war.'

The central role of the Sovereign in providing a focal point for
grieving and silent prayer for remembrance has continued
through another world war and others wars since then, to the
present reign. Thus in opening the Air Forces Memorial at
Runnymede on 17 October 1953, Queen Elizabeth II alluded to
Magna Carta and remarked:

> It is very fitting that those who rest in nameless graves should
> be remembered in this place. For it was in these fields of
> Runnymede seven centuries ago that our forefathers first
> planted a seed of liberty which helped to spread across the
> earth the conviction that man should be free and not enslaved.
>
> And when the life of this belief was threatened by the iron
> hand of tyranny, their successors came forward without
> hesitation to fight, and, if it was demanded of them, to die
> for its salvation. As only free men can, they knew the value of
> that for which they fought, and that the price was worth
> paying.
>
> For wherever and for as long as freedom flourishes on the
> earth, the men and women who possess it will thank them and
> will say that they did not die in vain. That is their true and
> everlasting memorial.

The Runnymede Memorial, designed by Sir Edward Maufe (who
also designed Guildford Cathedral) is a shrine to 20,000 service-
men and women who lost their lives flying from bases in the
United Kingdom and Northern and Western Europe in the
Second World War. The memorial is bounded by a cloister in
which the names of the dead are recorded, while coats of arms of
the Commonwealth countries are represented on the cloister
ceilings. Engraved on the great north window of the shrine are

words from the Psalm 139, often referred to as the 'Airman's Psalm':

> If I climb up into Heaven, Thou art there;
> If I go to Hell, Thou art there also.
> If I take the wings of the morning
> And remain in the uttermost parts of the sea,
> Even there also shall Thy hand lead me;
> And Thy right hand shall hold me.

Over 160,000 airmen sacrificed their lives in the air forces of the Commonwealth during the Second World War. These missing men and women are remembered through a series of memorials from around the world, in such places as El Alamein, Singapore, Ottawa and the island of Malta.

The Queen returned on 17 October 2003 for a service of commemoration, which concluded with a lone bagpiper playing a lament and a fly-past of four tornado aircraft from the RAF.

The Air Forces Memorial is only one of the many 2,500 war cemeteries and memorials built by The Commonwealth War Graves Commission, which was established by Royal Charter in 1917. Its task since then has been to pay tribute to the 1,700,000 service men and women of the Commonwealth forces who died in both world wars. One of its principles is that on a headstone 'there should be no distinction made on account of military or civil rank, race or creed'. Over 1 million casualties of war are now commemorated at military and civil sites in over 150 countries. HRH The Duke of Kent is its present Royal President.

Rudyard Kipling experienced personal tragedy with the death of his son, whom he had arranged to join the Irish Guards despite intial rejection on the grounds of poor eyesight, in 1915 at the Battle of Loos. He was to vent his feelings of guilt in the words, 'If any question why we died/ Tell them , because our fathers lied' and then went on to write the acclaimed 'My Boy Jack'. He joined Sir Fabian Ware's 'Imperial War Graves Commission' and it was Kipling who was responsible for suggesting the biblical wording 'Their Name Liveth For Evermore' found on the headstones in large war graves, and also

'Known Unto God' upon the headstones of those who remain unidentified. His short story 'The Gardener' involves visits to the war cemeteries.

Yet earlier in his hey day Kipling turned down an offer of appointment as Poet Laureate to Queen Victoria during the interregnum of the laureateship between 1892 and 1896, although there were unsubstanciated rumours that she disapproved of him in some way.

Falklands Remembrance

In May 1982 a total of 28,000 British service personnel headed to the South Atlantic to prosecute the Falklands War. By its successful conclusion a total of 255 were killed. This was less than in the Korean War, Malaya and Northern Ireland until 1982, but more than in Cyprus, Aden and Borneo. But such has been the change in attitude within society since the Korean War that the Ministry of Defence was obliged to repatriate most of the dead of the Falklands War to Britain, with only 23 bodies remaining buried in the Falklands at 'Blue Beach' Military Cemetery at San Carlos. Until then it had been the tradition to bury British service personnel killed overseas in whatever country or location they died on active service. Of the 88 Royal Naval personnel killed, many were lost at sea and have no grave except unmarked war wrecks, which the Royal Navy traditionally honour by flying the White Ensign underwater from wrecks identified as war graves. During the twenty-fifth anniversary commemorations of the Falklands War in 2007 HRH The Earl of Wessex represented The Queen in laying a wreath at Blue Beach, and on 16 June the McAulay family were flown over the site of the sinking of HMS *Ardent* in a Lynx helicopter from HMS *Edinburgh* from which a wreath was dropped.

Also present at the Drumhead Service Commemorations in the Falklands was the 'Cross of Nails', originally presented by Coventry Cathedral to HMS *Coventry* when commissioned, from which it had been retrieved by navy divers two months after its sinking and given to a veteran survivor who gifted it back to Coventry Cathedral. The royal family's role in facilitating and

HRH The Prince Edward, Earl Wessex, at Fitzroy, Falkland Islands, in 2007 remembering the 25th Anniversary of the War of 1982 (in which HRH The Prince Andrew flew with the Fleet Air Arm)

heading up such commemorations is a much valued aspect of military life.

Remembrance in South Africa

In 1999 The Queen and the Duke of Edinburgh visited South Africa over Remembrance Sunday and to coincide with this a special instruction was issued for the ceremony at Whitehall:

> This year at the end of the Last Post the massed bands of the Guards Division will play Berenice. During that time there will be television coverage of HM The Queen and HRH The Duke of Edinburgh laying wreaths in Durban earlier today. Following that The Prince of Wales and other members of the Royal Family will lay wreaths.

In Durban two hours earlier, The Queen and the Duke of
Edinburgh heard Jewish, Muslim and Hindu prayers offered, and
a Methodist minister, Darene Jordaan, read Christian prayers.
Following the ceremony The Queen and the Duke walked to St
Paul's Anglican Church for an act of worship. Having also a
wider responsibility as Head of State and of the Commonwealth
has enabled The Queen to respect and represent peoples of all
faiths, and none, at such ceremonies of remembrance without
compromising her personal belief or governorship of the Church
of England.

The National Memorial Arboretum (NMA), Alrewas, Staffordshire

This was opened by HRH The Duchess of Kent on 16 May 2001
on 82 acres of land from reclaimed gravel works along the River
Tame, then generously donated by Redland Aggregates, since
which a further 70 acres including the wildlife lake has also been
gifted by Redland's successor, Lafarge. The concept of honouring
service personnel killed since the Second World War came from
a visit to Arlington Cemetery and the National Arboretum in
Washington, DC, by David Childs in 1988. Prime Minister John
Major launched the appeal on the basis of the concept being so
worthy even before Redlands donated the land.

On 12 October 2007 the striking Armed Forces Memorial was
opened by The Queen, the Duke of Edinburgh, and the Prince of
Wales and Duchess of Cornwall, and dedicated by the Archbishop of Canterbury. Designed by Liam O'Connor, it honours
the 16,000 service personnel killed on active service, in terrorism
and in training since the Second World War, including those
caught up in conflicts and wars since 1 January 1948, following
on from the Commonwealth War Graves Commission brief
whose commemorations end with those who died on 31
December 1947, the one exception being those killed in
Palestine who are included on this memorial.

The Queen paused to look at the names of Earl Mountbatten,
her cousin, who was killed by a Provisional IRA bomb aboard his
boat in Northern Ireland in 1979. The public donated almost

£7million towards its creation, and in its official opening programme, the Prince of Wales observed that: 'The scale of this memorial is a poignant reminder to us all of the continuing cost of the democracy and freedom we enjoy, as well as the constant sacrifices being made on our behalf around the world.'

The dedication service by the Archbishop of Canterbury included hymns and a reading by the Duke of Edinburgh, followed by an RAF fly-past of nine aircraft spanning different decades familiar to those commemorated below:

Palestine 1945–48
Malaya 1948–60
Yangtze 1949
Korea 1950-53
Canal Zone 1951–54
Kenya 1952–1956
Cyprus 1955–1959
Suez 1956
Arabian Peninsula 1957–60
Congo 1964–69
Brunei 1962–64
Borneo 1962–66
Cyprus 1964 to present day
Radfan 1964
South Arabia 1964–67
Malay Peninsula 1964–65
Northern Ireland 1969–2007
Dhofar 1969–78
Rhodesia 1979–80
South Atlantic 1982
Lebanon 1983–84
Gulf of Suez 1984
Gulf 1988–89

Peshawar 1989–90
Namibia 1989-90
Gulf 1990–91
Kuwait 1991
Iraq/Kuwait 1991–2003
Western Sahara 1991 to present day
Northern Iraq/Southern Turkey 1991
Cambodia 1991–93
Former Yugoslavia 1992–2002
Sarajevo 1993–98
Georgia 1993 to present day
Rwanda 1993–98
Angola 1997
Croatia 1996–98
Kosovo 1998–2002
Sierra Leone 1999–2002
Congo 1999 to present day
Kosovo 1999–2007
East Timor 1999
Ethiopia and Eritrea 2000 to present day
Macedonia 2001–02
Afghanistan 2001 to present day
Iraq 2003 to present day

On 29 October 2008 HRH The Princess Royal and Vice Admiral Timothy Laurence went to Westminster Abbey to attend the dedication of a memorial to the Armed and Auxiliary Forces who have died in theatres of war since 1945. Designed by Tom Phillips the memorial is an 'integral metal plaque', the inscription reading: 'Remember the men and women of the Armed and Auxiliary Forces who have lost their lives in times and places of conflict since the Second World War'.

The Princess Royal tasked the Dean of Westminster with the words: 'Mr Dean, to remember the sacrifice and heroism in defence of freedom of the men and women who have lost their lives, I place this memorial in the custody of the Dean and Chapter and invite you to dedicate it.'

At the Service of Dedication that followed, lessons were read by Miss Kelly Thompson, youngest daughter of the late Senior Aircraftsman Gary Thompson, Royal Air Force Regiment, who was killed in Afghanistan in April 2008 (Josh. 4.1-9), and by HRH Princess Royal (Phil. 4.4–9).

Notes

[1] National Archives: CAB 24/C45.
[2] War Cabinet Peace Celebrations Committee, Draft Minutes of meeting 9 May 1919, 1-2 National Archives file: Cab 27/52.
[3] Royal Society of Arts Archive, Ref. PR/GE/117/10/14.

14

Royal Prayers of Diana, Princess of Wales

God our Father, we remember before you DIANA, Princess of Wales,
and offer you our gratitude for all the memories of her that we treasure still.
Her vulnerability and her willingness to reach out to the excluded and forgotten
touched us all; her generosity gave hope and joy to many.
May she rest in peace where sorrow and pain are banished,
and may the everlasting light of your merciful love shine upon her;
through Jesus Christ our Lord. Amen.

Father eternal, unfailing source of peace to all who seek you, we entrust to your love and protection all for whom this anniversary of the tragic and untimely death of Diana, Princess of Wales reawakens the pains of grief and loss. Comfort all who mourn, that casting all their cares upon you, they may be filled with your gifts – of new life, of courage and of hope; through Jesus Christ our Lord. Amen.

These two prayers of the Church of England were written by the Archbishop of Canterbury to mark the tenth anniverasry of the death of Diana, Princess of Wales.

Herein lie clues to the late Diana, Princess of Wales's method of delivering royal prayer. It was seldom vocalized, nor was the Almighty invoked publicly in traditional form before a course of action – albeit a formal opening of some charitable event or launching of an endeavour. Endeavouring to apply an ethos of compassion and to relieve the plight of the less fortunate among mankind of all ages and persuasions wherever they were to be found, while at the same time necessarily being fully immersed in the world and all its needs and temptations as a public figurehead, was a challenge set by the Princess of Wales. The task and ideal type of applicant was described nearly 2,000 years ago by the Apostle St James: 'Pure religion and undefiled before God and the father is this; to visit the fatherless and widows in their affliction, and to keep himself unspotted from the world' (James 1.27). While no one would claim to have managed the latter, the Princess of Wales certainly joins other members of the royal family scoring points with the former. Indeed, her gift in this respect was almost universally recognized around the globe.

It was standing in for an engagement that Queen Elizabeth the Queen Mother was (most unusually) unable to fulfil at Westminster Cathedral in aid of the Cardinal Hume Centre, a charity tackling homelessness, that afforded the Princess of Wales the opportunity of meeting Cardinal Hume. This was to result in her supporting the Cardinal's charities for the homeless throughout the rest of her life. At Emmanuel College, Cambridge, where she laid the foundation stone for a new library at the request of the Master, Lord St John of Fawsley, she was to meet and befriend in his causes the College Chaplain. His project to convert the crypt of St Pancras Church in London to become a shelter and advice centre for the homeless sleeping rough around railway termini captured her attention.

Her interests in the whole field of compassion took practical form in the royal patronages she undertook: These included the Great Ormond Street for Sick Children in London, the Royal Marsden Hospital, which specializes in the treatment of cancer, Centrepoint, an organization working with the homeless, the National Aids Trust and The Leprosy Mission – to name but some. The Princess's love of the arts led her to become Patron of the English National Ballet.

Her ability to break down prejudice and barriers of fear were symbolized by such actions as that described by former President of the United States, Bill Clinton, at the 2001 Princess of Wales Memorial Lecture on AIDS:

> In 1987, when so many still believed that AIDS could be contracted through casual contact, Princess Diana sat on the

sickbed of a man with AIDS and held his hand. She showed the world that people with AIDS deserve not isolation, but compassion and kindness. It helped change the world's opinion, and gave hope to people with AIDS.

A decade later, in January 1997, the Princess of Wales was to be seen in Angola, dressed in anti-flash helmet and flak jacket, in her determination to bring greater awareness about the continuing deployment and legacy of anti-personnel landmines. Even a few days before her death she was visiting Bosnia with the Landmine Survivors Network. Her own legacy was enshrined in the Foreign Secretary's speech to Parliament introducing the second reading of the 1998 Landmines Bill, and recommending the signing of the international Ottawa Treaty banning the use of anti-personnel mines:

> All Honourable Members will be aware from their postbags of the immense contribution made by Diana, Princess of Wales to bringing home to many of our constituents the human costs of landmines. The best way in which to record our appreciation of her work, and the work of NGOs that have campaigned against landmines, is to pass the Bill, and to pave the way towards a global ban on landmines.

Carol Bellamy, Executive Director of the United Nations Children's Fund (UNICEF) echoed the necessity to take action to save a new generation, saying they presented: 'a deadly attraction for children, whose innate curiosity and need for play often lure them directly into harm's way'. With the sudden death of Princess Diana, The Queen spoke for the nation when she broadcast her thoughts on the 5 September 1997, the eve of the Princess's funeral:

> I hope that tomorrow we can all, wherever we are, join in expressing our grief at Diana's loss, and gratitude for her all-too-short life. It is a chance to show to the whole world the British nation united in grief and respect. May those who died rest in peace and may we, each and every one of us, thank God for someone who made many, many people happy.

15

Royal Prayers in the Exploration of Earth and Space and the Development of Nuclear Theology

From Ming Statutes the words of the Chinese Emperor's prayers and meditations are known. He would enter the Tian Tian (Temple of Heaven), in company with a choir, and say:

> To Thee, O mysterious-working Maker, I look up in thought ... With great ceremonies, I reverently honour Thee ... Thy servant, I bow my head to the earth reverently, expecting Thine abundant grace. All my officers are here arranged along with me, joyfully worshiping before Thee.

This was followed by three days of fasting, and then sacrifices were made on a giant three tiered altar. In the Hall of Prayer for Good Harvests a throne was erected in the centre – not for the Emperor but to house a blue and gold plaque bearing the title 'One True God' called Huang Tian Shang Di (Ruler of Heaven, the Emperor Above). There were no images of Shang Di, to whom the earthy Emperor was himself subject, and his people in turn to him. The Emperor had to bow to the presence of Shang Di and had to offer blood sacrifices to acknowledge his earthly status. In Chinese characters the title of the temple of Tian Tian comprises the character for Heavenly Person, originally in its ancient form with a dot or tiny circle over the character for great, itself made up of a horizontal stroke (i.e. a picture character displaying arms outstretched meaning great person) above the symbol for person. The combined result is not a reference to an abstract idea but rather to a person who is 'Emperor Above'.

According to *The Overall Survey of the Ocean Shores*, a diary written by Ma Huan and published in 1433 after Zheng He's last voyage of discovery, in 1421 four great armadas of Chinese ships set sail to discover the world, the remnant returning to China in 1423.

The instigator was the new Emperor, Zhu Di, fourth son of Zhu Yuangzhang, who had risen from being the son of hired labourer in Mongol occupied China, by conquest to become the first Ming emperor in 1368, having expelled the last of Ghengis Khan's Mongol successors, Toghon Temor, and occupied the city of Ta Tu, formerly Kublai Khan's capital, later under Zhu Di in 1421 to become Beijing. The Emperor took the Dragon Throne with the title 'Emperor on Horseback, Son of Heaven'.

Many Mongol survivors were castrated following Zhu Di's military campaign, among them Ma He at Kunming. But he nevertheless proved to be loyal to the new Ming cause and was drafted to the royal household of Zhu Di, his name being changed at the same time to Zheng He. Like many of his fellow Mongol warriors, he was a devout Muslim.

Emperor Zhu Di was bent upon creating a huge maritime fleet to explore and plunder the world's resources. Although with no experience of the sea, Zheng He was appointed Commander-in-Chief of a fleet of 1,681 new ships, including 250 'treasure ships', massive nine-masted vessels built at the Longjiang Shipyards which dwarfed anything Western Europe was producing. Indeed just the rudder of one, at 36 feet in height, was not far short of the entire length of Columbus's *Nina*. And there were 3,500 other vessels.

The first of Zheng He's voyages, between 1405 and 1407, involved 62 'treasure ships' crewed and manned by 27,800 men, and explored as far as Calicut on the Indian coast. It was marked by an appeal to the 'Divine' during a ferocious storm, in which sailors prayed to Ma Tsu to save them from drowning and shipwreck. A 'Divine Light' (St Elmo's Fire?) appeared at the tips of the masts of Zhenh He's flagship and 'as soon as this miraculous light appeared, the danger was appeased'.

The sailors believed that the fleet was divinely ordained through the prayers of the Emperor – for the Dragon Throne represented the unification of heaven with earth, and herein lies the clue to use of Chinese maritime royal prayers. Every vessel in

Zheng He's fleet had a small cabin dedicated to Ma Tsu, the mariners' deity. Dressed in red, Ma Tsu would appear to sailors as a warning that unseen storms were rising and that their voyages should be postponed.

Prayers were offered to her every evening before supper, and whenever the crew put ashore in foreign lands, circular bronze mirrors were carried to deflect evil spirits, with the eight-spoked Taoist wheel depicted on the reverse of each one. As late as 1983 a stone head of Ma Tsu from Admiral Zhou Man's fleet voyage tasked with exploring the world west of South America beginning from the Falkland Islands at 52 degrees 40 minutes South as part of the great 1421–23 world exploration, was discovered in Australia beneath the beach at Milton, New South Wales. It is now in the Kedumba Nature Museum in Katoomba.

Although the Chinese great fleet had set sail from Tanggu following prayers offered to Ma Tsu, the reign of Zhu Di was characterized by religious tolerance. Aboard his ships were included Islamic, Hindu and Buddhist savants to minister to others aboard of these persuasions. On the great fleet voyages were to be found the Buddhist monk, Sheng Hui, and other religious leaders, Ha San and Pu Hi Ri. Confucianism was not seen as conflicting with Buddhism.

In addition to tantalizing records of Franciscan missionaries to China in the sixteenth century that spoke of Chinese expeditions in fleets of 60 to 100 ships sailing to what we now know is Australia, together with charts of that continent, recorded on sixth-century copper scrolls, now lost, there is much artefactual evidence of the great fleet voyages of 1421–23.

One sequence of such finds illustrates the discovery of the American Pacific seaboard coast by the great Chinese fleet in 1423. A shipwreck of teak, with elements consistent with a fifteenth century Chinese treasure ship, has been discovered off Neahkahnie Beach in Oregon. The surviving pulley for sail-hoisting was made of a wood unique to South East Asia, calophyllum, but has yet to undergo carbon dating. Other finds associated with the shipwreck include paraffin wax; a substance used in the inventories of Zheng He's great fleet for desalinating water for horses. Part of another wreck was discovered in the mouth of the Sacramento River in San Francisco Bay in the nineteenth century. A suit of medieval Chinese armour was retrieved from the hold, now sadly lost after its lending to a local school, while the rest of the wreck was buried under a heavy accumulation of river silt. Magnetometer readings revealed a hull 85 feet long and 30 wide, the size of a conventional trading junk accompanying Zheng's fleet. Fragments recovered are carbon dated to 1410. Most interestingly, fragments of wood and a compacted ball of seeds weighing 80 lbs was recovered. The wood is Keteleria, a conifer native to South East Asia but not North America, the ball of seeds is undergoing analysis at present and rice grains indigenous to Africa and China, but not America in the fifteenth century have been identified.

If such evidence serves to confirm the discovery of the American seaboard coast by the Chinese in 1423, it owed much to the celestial navigation skills of Zheng He's fleet under the command of Zhou Man. Emperor Zhu Di had resumed the nightly practice of recording the starry sky, identifying 1,400 stars as they traversed the night sky, as they set about complying with the Emperor's instruction to 'compare and correct the drawings of the guiding stars', essential for maritime navigation and the drawing of charts.

The religions aboard the Chinese fleets were not troubled by the discoveries of mankind on these distant shores, but Christians certainly were by news of Columbus's discovery of humankind on the Caribbean Islands of the Bahamas, Cuba and Hispaniola in 1492. As it happens Columbus took with him a chart, acquired through a circuitous route of provenance, and Gavin Menzies [1] has revealed its origin as having lain with Niccolo da Conti's (Bartholomew of Florence) involvement with the Chinese fleet and his bringing to Venice in 1424 a Chinese 'world' chart acquired from his years of service in the Chinese treasure fleet and his contact in India with the fleet that had explored the coasts of India, Africa to Cape Verde (where they left a stone still extant inscribed in Malayalam as spoken in Kerrala near Calicut whence the Chinese fleet had sailed), the Falklands Islands, Australia and China.

In his 1974 analysis of Columbus's 'Diario/Log', for which he was awarded a doctorate by the University of Cadiz in 1979, Dr Luis Coin, himself a master mariner, posited that Columbus deliberately falsified his 'public' log to suggest he had charted a course much further north than the one he actually sailed (and subsequently followed) deep into Portuguese waters where he would have faced death if captured at his outset. Clues include Columbus's complaint that he had met contrary currents but which do not exist west of the Canaries, and would have been against him anyway had he then headed south; the existence of less salty water near the outset as noted by his crew (a sign of proximity to the African coast); the hooking of tuna which are not prevalent west of the Canaries; noting of mats of Sargasso weed; mid-ocean sightings of a pelican and a duck (impossible unless near islands such as Cape Verde). That Columbus had the use at least of the Florentine Paolo Toscanelli's chart is evidenced by his correspondence of 1481–82 in which Toscanelli observed:

> I notice your splendid and lofty desire to sail to the regions of the East by those of the West as is shown by the chart which I send you, which would be better shown in the shape of a round sphere ... not only is the said voyage possible, but it is sure and certain, and of honour and countless gain ... I have had most fully the good and true information ... of other merchants who have long trafficked in those parts, men of great authority.

This chart showed the westward route to the new world via Antilia. The link in all this was Da Conti who had sailed with the Chinese fleet and had drawn a chart based on the Chinese voyages of 1421 to 1423 which he now chose to share not only with Toscanelli and thus Columbus, but also with Behain of Bohemia, who placed a copy in the Portuguese Treasury. There Magellan admitted he had seen it before setting out on his voyage. The strait between the Atlantic and Pacific Oceans that was to bear his name was already marked on it.

The immediate problem Columbus's discoveries posed for Christians was how was the existence of men on hitherto 'undiscovered' shores to be reconciled with the words in Genesis, indicating a Garden of Eden in the Western world as the origin of mankind?

The matter would have been less theologically challenging had Columbus and others in their lifetime owned up to having used information from the Chinese fleets which indicated earlier contact with mankind around the globe. Trading could have sufficed as an explanation for the means by which mankind had been displaced until genetics revealed 'prehistoric' migrations across continents and seas.

It took the French Protestant scholar, Isaac La Peyrère (1594–1676) to effect that reconciliation by means of proposing an interpretation of Genesis incorporating a pre-Adamite creation in God's image at Gen. 1.27. This brilliant proposal liberated historians at a stroke, for it meant that they were not bounden to ignore or 'bend' the fact of the existence of ancient civilizations described in surviving architecture as they emerged from writings of China and Classical Greece. It also explained how people who were not in Adam's family came to be mentioned in the story of Cain and his punishment. But while the 'Two-Creations' theory allowed scientists a free rein, it also led to the unintended and most appalling consequences for racial harmony and anti-Semitism that provided dark undercurrents in the American Civil War, two World Wars and some conflicts which extend to the present day.

The papacy fought rearguard actions in defence of inadequate tenets challenged by the findings of astronomers such as Galileo and Copernicus, eventually succumbing and joining the age of discovery through the construction of papal observatories: the Observatory of the Roman College (1774–1878), the Observatory of the Capitol (1827–70), and the Specula Vaticana (1789–1821) in the Tower of the Winds within the Vatican. The British royal family have a largely unheralded but fearless and spectacular record of promoting such frontier discovery, and by this means have exposed narrow and bigoted minds as insupportable in the face of man's place in a much greater picture of existence.

King Charles II had established the Royal Observatory on Greenwich Hill in 1675 for exactly the same reasons as Zhu Di had ordered the resumption of nightly stellar observation in China in the 1420s, the order to Flamsteed in the Royal Warrant of 22 June 1675 reading: 'to apply himself with the most exact care and diligence to the rectifying of the tables of the motions of the heavens, and the places of the fixed stars, so as to find out the so much desired longitude of places for the perfecting of the art of navigation', while a subsequent Royal Warrant in 1675 ordered the construction of the Royal Observatory. In 1720 George I appointed Edmund Halley as Flamsteed's successor, establishing him as 'Our Astronomical Observator in Our Observatory at Greenwich', although the first royal visit to the observatory was by Queen Caroline in 1727.

In the same vein, but with the determination to encourage the exploration of space as an outward venture, King George III in 1768 ordered Chambers to build an observatory in Richmond capable of observing the forthcoming transit of Venus set for 3 June 1769. By means of this, it was theorized that the scale of the solar system could be calculated when Earth, Venus and the Sun were more of less in a straight line. King George III also ordered Captain James Cook to voyage to Tahiti in the Pacific to observe the transit of Venus from there to aid in such calculations. The result was to prove that the Solar System was ten times larger than previously thought in the Western world, and to pose questions about the possibility of life forms beyond Earth. King George III's patronage of the German astronomer William Hershel was to demolish the known understanding of the solar system as comprising the sun and six planets. Hershel discovered Uranus on 13 May 1781. His work led to galactic theory and modern theories of the universe.

In 1782 King George III invited Hershel to bring his telescope to an audience in Windsor Castle, and then paid £4,000 for the construction of the largest telescope of its day with a 40-foot focal and aperture of 49 inches, sited in a field in Slough. Hershel was to describe George III to Sir Joseph Banks as 'the best of Kings, who is the liberal protector of every art and science' – even proposing to call his newly discovered planet 'Georgium Sidus'. Yet such scientific discovery has not served to relegate royal prayer to the dustbin of history. Christianity has subsequently gone hand-in-hand with such discoveries and advances, largely because the royal family have by means of their liberal patronage caused, or even forced, Christian interpretation and ethics to evolve with such advances. Christian prayer might seem to be an unlikely bedfellow of the royal family and scientists, but all three are to be found in the daily rounds and lives of the royal family today. Nowadays there are two Astronomers Royal, the second title being Astronomer Royal for Scotland which was created in 1834.

With the same intensions as King George III, the Prince of Wales on 28 April 2003 visited the Radio Telescope Observatory at Jodrell Bank in Cheshire to commemorate the £2.5 million upgrade of the 76-metre dish, now named in honour of Sir Bernard Lovell who had overseen its original conception and construction between 1955 and 1959, to give it a new surface enabling it to operate at a range of frequencies four times greater than hitherto in its analysis of deep space.

HRH The Prince of Wales at Jodrell Bank in 2003 with Sir Bernard Lovell and Professor Andrew Lyne

The onset of the 'space race' has brought with it an unintentional parallel threat to the very existence of mankind. And so the ethics of royal prayer to prevent this misuse have remained relevant. The cosmic battles described and foreseen in the Book of Revelation still seem relevant as mankind now sees further into the cosmic battleground and carries religion with it.

Ironically, the main driving components of the great dish at Jodrell Bank employed gear racks rescued from the scrapping of the 18-inch gun turret racks from the battleships HMS *Royal Sovereign* and HMS *Revenge* at Inverkeithing in 1949 – ironic because HMS *Revenge* had served off Greek waters in 1922–23 during the abdication crisis which toppled King Constantine I and led to Prince Philip coming to Britain and the visit of his son, the Prince of Wales, to Jodrell Bank in 2003. It had been aboard HMS *Revenge* in 1919 that Von Reuter escaped punishment by explaining his actions in ordering the scuttling of the 74 ships of the German High Seas Fleet that had surrendered in Scapa Flow, remarking: 'I am convinced that any English Naval Officer, placed as I was, would have acted in the same way.' Much unexpected good has come of Von Reuter's decision, for since the Hiroshima bomb metal from the radioactive-free scuttled German High Seas Fleet has been raised from time to time to provide the means to construct sensitive scientific instruments, primarily in the field of oncology treatment. And so members of the royal family have found themselves opening and dedicating medical units equipped from this unexpected source.

Even stranger, is the contribution of HMS *Royal Sovereign* whose gun gear racks became such an integral part of the 76-metre telescope at Jodrell Bank, for she had been loaned to the USSR in 1944 for convoy duties, operating out of Murmansk and Arckhangelsk as the *Archangels*. In an interview with 'Space.uk' Sir Bernard Lovell recalled the task of Jodrell Bank in response to the perceived threat of the launch of the world's first satellite into space by the USSR:

> Sputnik was launched on 4th October 1967 and I had no intention of doing anything about it until I had a telephone

call from the [Government] Director of Guided Weapons who said there was no instrument in the western world that could detect the launching rocket, which we knew was the world's first intercontinental missile ... we equipped the telescope with a transmitter and had the good fortune to get a most incredible echo from the carrier rocket of the *Sputnik*.

In fact the Mark1 telescope tracked the third stage of the carrier rocket by radar. Demonstrating its defence use as a unique instrument to track the telemetry of United States and USSR satellites, and to monitor those sent further afield into the solar system, it also found its use in February 1966 when tracking the USSR unmanned Moon lander *Luna 9*, poaching its facsimile transmission of photographs from the moon's surface and gaining the same photographs.

With intercontinental ballistic missiles deployed both on land and beneath the sea aboard submarines, and the Cuban missile crisis demonstrating how close humanity has come to destruction, the Cold War stand-off was aptly summarized in the 1977 James Bond movie. *The Spy Who Loved Me*, when Commander Bond, briefly under arrest, is enjoined to watch a radar screen charting the trajectory of two intercontinental ballistic missiles loosed off by rogue submarines at cities on different continents with the comment: 'Behold, Mr Bond, the instruments of Armageddon'. Yet such weaponry also preserved the peace, and so the place of royal prayer in the blessing of the use of such warships for the benefit of mankind against evil intent has become ever more important.

Dr Charles Elliott remarked in debate with Canon David Edwards of Westminster through a column in *Crucible* (journal of the Church of England's Board for Social Responsibility) in reply to his report on 'The State of the Nation' in 1976: 'If all theology can do is sprinkle holy water on our secular judgements, or give a brief nod in the Almighty's direction as a kind of coda, then it is not to be taken seriously'. The dedicated application of royal prayer in the midst of ethical dilemmas supplies just that missing theology where the ethics of scientific application is so vulnerable, and where theology could so easily be absent.

The world was made even more insecure through the betrayal to the USSR of the technology employed from 1941 in what became the Manhattan Project, to construct the nuclear bomb by members of the British 'Cambridge 5' ring of spies.

Joining the Foreign Office in 1936, John Cairncross, apart from his more famous surreptitious dealings at Bletchley Park, from 1941 betrayed the technology behind 'Tube Alloys' as Private Secretary to Lord Hankey – the Anglo-American atomic bomb project, known as 'Manhattan' in the USA. Soviet Head of Intelligence, Pavel Fitin, commented upon Cairncross's contribution to 'Enormoz' (i.e. the USSR's endeavour to uncover the West's atomic technology):

> Extremely valuable information on the scientific developments of Enormoz reaches us from London Rezidentura. The first material was received at the end of 1941 from John Cairncross. This material contained valuable and highly secret documentation, both the essence of the Enormoz problem and on the measures taken by the British government to organize and develop work on atomic energy. This material formed the point of departure for building the basis of, and organizing the work on, the problem of atomic energy in our country.

In 1944 Donald Maclean was posted to Washington as First Secretary in the British Embassy and used that entrée to examine and pass to the Soviets yet more secrets of atomic technology as well as private communications between Truman and Churchill, while Alan May Nunn, who had worked from 1942 at the Cambridge Cavendish Laboratories on the atomic project, and then in Canada on the same project, actually stole potentially fatal samples of uranium 233 and 235 and handed them across to his Soviet 'control' to be flown to Moscow.

Spying for the Soviet Union from time to time became curiously juxtaposed with elements of history, including royal prayer, that stood for Britain. Unaware of his Soviet allegiance Anthony Blunt was innocently appointed Surveyor of the King's Pictures following the conclusion of the Second World War. He was allocated two offices at the rear of the Grand Staircase of the State Apartments at St James's Palace, from where he would visit

Kensington Palace on the pretext of examining the paintings there, only to cross the Paddock and deposit copies of secret documents and photographs of others at the Soviet Embassy opposite for onward transmission to Moscow.

Blunt's arrival at St James's Palace missed by a whisker the vacation of adjacent offices occupied by Major Frank Foley, British Passport Control Officer in Berlin in 1939 as the war loomed, who helped thousands of Jews to escape Nazi Germany. Foley was to end up leading the Norwegian resistance and then returning to London to interrogate Rudolph Hess (Foley being a perfect German speaker) at Mytchett Manor. Foley in May 1942 took over the top secret 'XX Committee' (Double Cross) which ran all double agents operated by Britain in Europe from offices initially in MI6's Section V's Department in St Albans, and from mid-1942 in St James's Street and Ryder Street. In the course of the war the XX Committee met a total of 226 times at their weekly meetings, beginning on 2 January 1941. The King, knowing something of Major Foley's secret work, offered him offices also in the more secure and discreet environment of St James's Palace.[2] Foley is on record as suspecting as early as November 1941 that Kim Philby's loyalties were in question. It was occasioned by accepting an invitation to stay at a colleague's landlady's house in St Albans in a spare bedroom overnight. Philby lived in the same road and the intention was for them all to meet, but Foley wished to avoid him. Foley's colleague remarked of Foley: 'He already had his suspicions, or maybe I should say "feelings", and during the course of the evening, he asked me – his words – "How well do you know Philby?". It was only later of course that I realised the significance of this remark.'[3]

Philby's fellow Soviet spy, Anthony Blunt, was at that time working in military intelligence in 'B Division' and working alongside B(1)a in the same room as Ultra decrypts were analysed, from which Blunt was able to 'see' how effectively Double Cross operations were operating. Blunt betrayed huge numbers of them, enabling some key German agents XX operatives to be 'turned' and run as Soviet-run Triple-Cross agents. Blunt regularly met Leo Long and other spies to receive and pass on information at Rainer's Snack Bar in Jermyn Street, near MI5's offices in 58 St James's Street. When Blunt left MI5 in 1945 he remarked to Colonel T.A. Robinson: 'Well, it has given me great pleasure to pass on the names of every MI5 officer to the Russians.'[4] Colonel Robinson reported the remark which was dismissed as flippancy, but it turned out to be true. Had Major Foley retained his offices at St James's Palace at the close of the war in 1945 it can only be imagined what damage to national security across Europe could have been wrought by the presence of Blunt, literally next door, from 1946, as the work of spies became so important to the unfolding of the Cold War.

When 'Operation Stop Watch' – the plan to build a secret tunnel for a quarter of a mile under Berlin to reach a cable housing over 300 lines that serviced several Soviet military bases – was conceived in 1954 within the walls of Number 2 Carlton Gardens, the headquarters of Section Y (MI6 Soviet Intercepts Division), they were betrayed by George Blake who had been assigned to take notes of the meeting. He went straight to his Soviet controller, Nikolai Rodin, but the Soviets kept quiet until 11 months after the tunnel became operational, when Colonel Vadim Goncharov 'discovered' the tunnel. Blake was eventually exposed in 1960, imprisoned but escaped from Wormwood Scrubs to Moscow in 1966. Strange then, that Operation Stop Watch had been conceived in what had been Lord Kitchener's house at Number 2 Carlton Gardens, who in 1914 had fronted the famous poster pointing and exclaiming 'Join Your Country's Army' with the royal prayer as its subscript 'God Save The King'.[5]

Yet the royal family have kept pace with all the machinations surrounding atomic developments, and continue to acquaint themselves of the consequences of each advance. As early as 1958 Queen Elizabeth II invited to Balmoral Castle a group of nuclear scientists from the Commonwealth Conference of nuclear scientists, and on 28 September was pictured in the gardens conversing with Shri M.R. Srinavsan, senior research officer of the engineering division of the Atomic Energy Establishment, Trombay, India, Dr G.L. Miles, director of the chemistry division of the Australian Atomic Energy Commission, and Dr Nazir Ahmad, Chairman of the Pakistan Atomic

Energy Commission. Royal prayer at opening of establishments

The Queen at Balmoral on 20 September 1958 hosting nuclear scientists, with (from left to right) Shri M.R. Srinivasan (senior research officer, engineering division Atomic Energy Establishment, Trombay, India), Dr G.L. Miles (leader of the Chemistry Section, Australian Atomic Energy Commission) and Dr Nazir Ahmad (chairman, Pakistan Atomic Energy Commission), all of whom were invited to lunch and discussion

employing peaceful uses of this energy has gone hand in hand with the continuance of royal prayer for the justifiable use of such energy as a means of deterrence of aggression, and for self-defence. It is manifest in royal prayers still employed at the launching of ships, aircraft and other technologies. Such prayers, though, are no empty remnant of the past; rather ,they are offered from a position of knowledge and recognition of the need to maintain their ethical use as enjoined by Christian principles.

Royal prayer associated with the launching and dedicating of weaponry for right usage is a completely ignored aspect of what is known as 'nuclear theology' – but it puts at rest the minds of ordinary soldiers, sailors and airmen who would otherwise have no ally in their ethical consciences. 'Nuclear theology' was first devised as a concept necessary to regulate the worst potential consequences of nuclear conflict, and Bernard Brodie of Yale University traces its evolution from 1946.

The ethical issues involved came to a head during the Cuban missile crisis from 14 to 28th October 1962, in which the President Khrushchev of the Soviet Union had secretly arranged for tactical nuclear missiles to be hidden in caves in Cuba months before sending a fleet of ships to Cuba carrying various components of nuclear weaponry for aiming at the nearby USA. Khrushchev was determined to 'put a hedgehog down Kennedy's pants' and to 'see just what he is made of'. Orders were issued to accompanying Soviet submarines to fire upon any USA warship that stopped a surface ship. Soviet submarines loaded nuclear torpedoes and cleared for battle, and Khruyschev threatened, 'If the USA insists on war then we'll all meet in hell'. The USA was unaware of the Soviet nuclear torpedo technology. This was extreme theology, but accurate given the Soviets' knowledge of the potential consequences of their actions.

What the Soviets did not know was that the USA's warships were equipped with nuclear depth charges. Chief of naval operations, Admiral George A. Anderson, in describing Navy preparedness for action as Soviet submarines approached the 'picket line of quarantine' in the Atlantic, recalled: 'We knew where one of these particular submarines was located ... We had a destroyer sitting on top of this submarine'.[6] At the same time a Soviet Zampolit (political adviser) aboard the submarine wet himself and feinted at hearing the Soviet Captain order the loading of nuclear torpedoes. On 25 October 1962 the US Navy aircraft photographed the first Soviet submarine to surface near the quarantine line.[7] It turned out to be a Soviet 'F' class submarine with conning tower number 945, and Soviet Fleet Number 3-130, commanded by Captain Shumkov. On 27 October Cuban anti-aircraft guns opened fire on low-level USA reconnaissance aircraft over the San Cristobel Soviet missile site, and the next day the US Navy was compelled to drop signal depth charges around a second Soviet F-class submarine to force

it to the surface. The world was indeed on the brink and within

'October 25, 1962: US Navy Surveillance of the first Soviet F-Class submarine to surface near quarantine line (conning tower number 945, Soviet fleet number B-130, commanded by Shumkov', Dino A Brugioni Collection, The National Security Archive at the George Washington University. Permission to publish is stated by objectives of the Archive; namely to place de-classified evidence in the public domain for international historical analysis in a freely available form

seconds of a nuclear war. The whole episode had massive repercussions for the development of 'nuclear theology'.

In the UK the Sovereign managed to impose an ethical requirement of a kind by the royal family's continuing practice of blessing warships, and interestingly the USA felt this need and continued to do the same. Thus, within a year after the Cuban missile crisis, President Woodrow Wilson's grandson, the Very Revd. Francis B. Sayre Jr, Dean of Washington Cathedral, delivered the following dedicatory prayer at the launch of the Sub-Surface, Ballistic Nuclear (SSBN) submarine, the USS *Woodrow Wilson*, armed with 16 of the latest version of Polaris strategic nuclear missiles, in 1963:

Polaris is a nuclear weapon of mass destruction. But ethically, the millionth A Bomb is no worse than the first. I decided that if Woodrow Wilson had lived today, the course of world history would have driven him to the Polaris submarine. I think he would have approved putting his name on that ship. I give you the prayer.[8]

Polaris could deliver a 500 kT warhead over a 1,500 mile trajectory, but there exists a rare and most fascinating account by Frank McFarlane, at the time 'Tool, Instrument Maker and Inspector for Lawrence [while] component parts were being made urgently in order to adapt our submarines for the reception of Polaris Missiles and to ensure the accurate delivery of the "thing" on target'. McFarlane wrestled with the ethics of working on such an endeavour, deep underground in the caverns beneath the city of Bath, known as HMS *Copenacre*.

> Fearful stuff indeed, one could have a clean or a dirty bomb, the latter although cheaper to produce would spread disaster for many miles around the target area and result in slow cancerous death for thousands of souls; the former would not be quite so deadly and would be much more likely to contain the evil within a small area, but the cost! I never knew what manner of bomb the submarine ultimately carried, which is perhaps as well.[9]

McFarlane decided that he would continue to develop the necessary guidance instrumentation on the basis of the lesser of two evils. This was the forerunner of the issue posed by the technology that soon enabled the nuclear powers to 'grade' a terrifying response.

Ethical questions arose about just where and when a nuclear response could, and most importantly *should*, be an option in the face of aggression. A dispassionate chart of logical response to this quadrille of options had to be devised. Questions arose about the fitness of politicians to decide such responses to threat and counter-threat – known as the 'Graduated Response' – replacing the massive one-off annihilation option (Mutual Assured Destruction). The USA devised the SIOP (Single Integrated Operational Plan) to deal with any tactical or strategic nuclear situation that might arise, but there was nothing in this 'nuclear theology' that addressed Divine presence, or absence.

It has been down to royal prayer at the launching of such nuclear vessels in the United Kingdom to address this neglected aspect, but one so important to her crews and their ethical consciences.

It is the monarch who enters the realms of nuclear theology once government and Parliament have made their democratic decisions of policy and it is the monarch who picks up the ethical dilemmas that now lie beyond those who have made the decisions. It is the monarch who is left to appeal to the Almighty through royal prayer for the right usage of the instruments of Armageddon.

Notes

1 G. Menzies, *1421 The Year China Discovered the World* (London: Transworld, 2003).

2 Author's correspondence 1997–99 with Frank Foley's cousin, William Urban, of Presque Isle, Maine, USA: 'of course my cousin didn't occupy only St James's Palace – he divided his time between there and Bletchley Park ... Fleming got his ideas for James Bond from his work in MI6'. When in London Foley lived in Nell Gwynne House, Sloane Avenue, a 'safe-house' opposite Chelsea Cloisters.

3 Unattributed quotation from secret service interviewee in M. Smith, *Foley: The Spy Who Saved 10,000 Jews* (London: Hodder and Stoughton, 1999), pp. 234–5.

4 Quoted in C. Pincher, *Their Trade is Treachery* (London: Sidgwick and Jackson, 1981), p. 102. Chapman Pincher remarks: 'Robertson, who says he knew that Blunt was a Communist and made no secret of it, passed on the information to those who should have taken note of it, but nothing was entered in Blunt's file', p. 103.

5 Kitchener Poster, Imperial War Museum Catalogue Number: IWM PST 2734.

6 Admiral G.W. Anderson, *Oral History Reminiscences, Vol. 2* (Annapolis MD: US Naval Institute, 1983), pp. 558–9.

7 National Security Archive, George Washington University, 'Submarine approaching 'Quarantine Line', 1962', Photograph Number 28.

8 Quotation of Dean Francis Sayre at the launch of USS *Woodrow Wilson*

on 22 February 1963, contained within *USS* Woodrow Wilson *SSBN 624, Official Commissioning Program* of 27 December 1963.

[9] F. McFarlane, *This I'll Defend – Loch Sloy* (London: privately published, 1990), p. 2. 'Of all things invented by man to secure instant death Polaris must rank supreme. I have already hinted at clean and dirty bombs but whether the appropriate department ever decided the content of the submarines equipped for Polaris Missile delivery the ships were designed to deliver the "goods" on target with devastating accuracy? To get to HMS Copenacre, the journey was by zig-zag car ride to the "pub", where the high rankers changed from their gold ringed uniforms into "civvies", any old shabby thing would do, as we completed our final journey in an old motor car ... there I close down on the most secret site the world has ever seen' pp. 4–5.

16

Epilogue: Royal Prayers – The Way Ahead

If, therefore, you value your thrones and your sceptres, you rulers of the nations, you must honour wisdom, so that you may reign for ever. (The Wisdom of Solomon)[1]

The association of royalty with religion has often led to much sneering from those purporting to represent the 'certainties' of science. Indeed, such a position has sometimes become institutionalized in the editorial stance of professional journals.

Atheism has frequently become the standard-bearer for such scientists. Not so for the monarchy. Why?

Royalty in the Old World has been aware of nearly every step along the scientific past – at times actually themselves instigating such advances, if not encouraging them (the examples of Henry the Navigator and George III are cases in point). In a curious way ancient monarchy has been around for long enough to see the certainties of science in their age become the stuff of yesterday; overtaken in turn by superior explanations of a more demonstratively (or theoretically) persuasive kind.

The same is happening again in our generation, witnessed by an interested monarchy. The 'certainties' of Darwin's 'Tree of Life' explanation with regard to the evolution of species, comprising only the multi-cellular specimens known to him, is now being challenged by the evidence of DNA, RNA and HGT. It was the discovery of DNA structure by Francis Crick in 1953 that led to the study of molecular evolution. That and the study of other biomolecules such as RNA and proteins that followed in its wake should, according to Darwin's theories, have confirmed the 'Tree' principle. This held that each branch spreading out from the trunk represented a single species for Darwin who drew such a tree in his red leather notebook, headed 'I think', in July 1837. Further branching points on his branches represent where one species becomes two. While most branches end in mid-air, indicating their extinction, others reach to the top, representing living species. For Darwin the tree was able to explain logically how every species was related to all others back to the origin of life, where is to be found the LUCA (last universal common ancestor). As Darwin in *On the Origin of Species* put it: 'the affinities of all the beings of the same class have sometimes been represented by a giant tree. I believe this simile largely speaks the truth'.

However, subsequent discoveries in the 1990s in the field of DNA sequencing of bacterial and archaean genes have not confirmed the RNA tree.[2] It is now possible to demonstrate that closeness in DNA terms might, to the contrary, be far removed in RNA terms. Thus the starfish (Luidia sarsi) can be defined as two species at once: one forming its larvae, and another the adult. Instead of degenerating, the larva of the starfish, once it has settled on the seabed and disgorged the miniature starfish from within its body, then itself swims off and lives another life as an independent animal for several months.

Are there two species involved, or just one? Which is correct as an explanation? The answer would now appear to be both – but only at the expense of Darwin's tree. Central to the integrity of Darwin's 'Tree of Life' is its 'vertical' characteristic, whereby organisms pass traits down to their offspring. This continues to be accepted and is still widely championed by such advocates as Peer Bork in his 2006 study at the European Biology Laboratory in Heidelberg. Others, such as Tal Dagan and William Martin of the Heinrich Heine University in Dusseldorf, have conducted studies that now differ. They can demonstrate that species frequently swap genetic material with other species, mostly through the medium of bacterial intrusion. This field of science is known as horizontal gene transfer (HGT). It is further complicated by endosymbiosis. The upshot is the realization that such insects as the fruit fly contain the entire genome of the bacterium Wolbachia, in effect rendering it a fly-bacterium chimera hybrid, rather than the simple fly we thought it was.

The ability of humans to form a placenta originated in a virus, syncytin, while cows contain snake DNA that transferred horizontally 50 million years ago. On some estimates up to 50 per cent of the human genome comprises DNA imported by viruses. Perhaps Darwin's 'Tree' explains the evolutionary origins of about 51 per cent of life, and may be valuable as that? But we now need something more in addition to accompany his inspired evolutionary theory, as the sheer complexity of life forms is beginning to be appreciated. Dr Rose in January 2009 opined in the *New Scientist*: 'The tree of life is being politely buried, we all know that. What's less accepted is that our whole fundamental view of biology needs to change'.[3] Graham Lawton (features editor of the *New Scientist*) comments upon this: 'if he is right, the tree concept could become biology's equivalent of Newtonian mechanics'.[4] Simon Conway Morris (Professor in the Department of Earth Sciences at Cambridge University) sees a larger picture: 'Darwin got it right, and so did Newton. But then physics had Einstein. Perhaps now its biology's turn.'[5] The 'certainties' of scientific conclusion are changing again. What might these new and unheeded developments mean for the respondents to a national UK survey in March 2009 by Theos, the public-theology think-tank, 37 per cent of whom thought that evolution removed the need for God?

Other 'givens' in Earth sciences are being overtaken by further discoveries and theories. For example, Drs Silver and Behn of the Carnegie Institution presented geological evidence in 2008 that plate tectonic movement of crustal plates between continents and beneath oceans, and volcanic activity, ceased altogether about 1 billion years ago for a significant period of time while all the continents were largely adjacent. Silver concludes: 'If plate tectonics indeed starts and stops, then continental evolution must be viewed in an entirely new light, since it dramatically broadens the range of possible evolutionary scenarios.' Tectonic cessation must have had a bearing upon the stages of evolution of life in its various forms.

However, cessation of tectonic movement is difficult to reconcile with the process explained by Albert Einstein in 1953 in the Foreword to a work[6] by Professor Charles Hapgood positing a theory of occasional total 'global crustal shift' brought about by the uneven distribution of continents, sometimes as little as 30 miles thick, which slides over the viscous underlayer of the Earth known as the asthenosphere. Einstein's explanation in support of Hapgood concluded that 'His idea is original, of great simplicity, and, if it continues to prove itself, of great importance to everything that is related to the history of the Earth's surface', and directed at the position of Antarctica over time, Einstein reasoned that the centrifugal force of the Earth's rotation acts on 'unsymetrically deposited masses, and produces centrifugal momentum that is transmitted to the rigid crust of the Earth ... and this will displace the polar regions towards the equator'. Such global crustal movement 'derived from the Earth's momentum of rotation ... will in turn tend to alter the axis of rotation of the Earth's crust'.[7]

It is not easily to appreciate, then, given the centrifugal forces calculated by Einstein as involved in the Earth's rotation, how the conglomeration of adjacent continents known to geologists as 'Rodinia', was able to stay together for as long as the genetic record of evolution of life forms would suggest before continents were split up and redistributed around the globe.

Then there is Professor Wickramasinghe's suggestion that life was seeded from viruses whose origins lay in space rather than Earth. Professor of Applied Mathematics and Astronomy at Cardiff University, and Director of the Cardiff Centre for Astrobiology Chadra Wickramasinghe worked with Sir Fred Hoyle on the infrared spectra of interstellar grains, leading to the modern theory of 'Panspermia' which proposes that cosmic dust in interstellar space and in comets is partly organic. He maintains that life on Earth was 'seeded' from space rather than arising through abiogensis. There is also the new reasearch into cosmic particle electron-volt damage to DNA resulting in life-form mutation. This would suggest that certain chartacteristics or abilities appear in animal and plant life as a result of intervention from space, having entirely bypassed but adding to the process of characteristics inherited through natural selection (D.J.P. Baldwin, in *Astronomy Now*). If this is the case and viruses and other organic life have drifted to Earth from space, then looking for an ultimate single origin of life on Earth may be a search based upon a false premise. On this basis we should instead be expanding our efforts to determine the origin of life beyond our planet's surface to find such organic determinants.

Cognizant of the immense significance such science, albeit sometimes at odds with other discoveries, royalty has recognized the achievements of great scientists and the advancement of science in their time. The means by which this has been achieved of late is membership of the Sovereign's Order of Merit.

One such member was Professor Francis Crick, J. W. Kieckhefer Distinguished Research Professor at the Salk Institute for Biological Studies in La Jolla, California. As co-discoverer of DNA, in 1953 Crick was made Member of the Order of Merit by Queen Elizabeth II.

Crick once joked, 'Christianity may be OK between consenting adults in private but should not be taught to young children', and in his book *Of Molecules and Men* he posed the question, at what point during biological evolution did the first organism have a soul, and at what moment does a baby acquire a soul? Crick denied the existence of a non-material soul that invested the body once created and then left at death, dismissing the cocncept as pure imagination. He also advocated that Darwinian natural selection be taught in school instead of religious education. He himself held 'a strong inclination towards atheism' and only accepted a fellowship at Churchill College in 1960 because it did not have a chapel, and resigned in protests when the college decided to build one.

In October 1969, Crick participated in a celebration of the one hundredth year of the journal *Nature*, advocating a new study of what he termed 'biochemical theology'. Crick wrote: 'So many people pray that one finds it hard to believe that they do not get some satisfaction from it', but then went on to suggest that his DNA studies led him to the conclusion that chemical molecular changes in the brain are really what constitute prayer, which itself is merely therefore the result of neurotransmitter and neurohormonal functions, with nothing supernatural involved.

Crick was thus effectively seduced by the results of his own research into denying the existence of forces invoked beyond the body, but he could not explain the effectiveness of prayer in altering actions beyond the material body itself whose chemical structures, for him, constituted the absolute boundary of scientific explanation of prayer. He had no explanation for the prayer of one person seeming to affect the circumstances of another.

He might have been interested in the field of quantum entanglement as an explanation, but that science now insisits upon a 'contact' of a kind between particles across micro or macro space.[8] Entanglement involves action at a distance in which two 'particles' behave synchronously with no apparent intermediary – a property known as 'non-local'. With this, gone are the confines of the human body in its living corporate form as a satisfactory explanantion for all that goes on in the religious human mind. Wave functions associated with quantum entanglement can operate across vast distances, seemingly 'communicating' simultaneously, in defiance of the present explanations of Einsteinian physics. Why should the human brain be singled out and excluded from hosting such quantum phenomena in order to insist upon the death of God?

Victor Stenger in *Quantum Gods: Creation, Chaos and the Search for Cosmic Consciousness,*[9] states there is no evidence for the brain operating quantum mechanically, arguing that the scale of distances involved in brain processing is in excess of a thousand times too large for quantum effects to come into play. In other words, prayer cannot operate quantum mechanically. However, in arguing that the brain is of the wrong scale to work quantum mechanically, Stenger would have to maintain that quantum mechanics works in isolation from, and has no interaction with, larger-scale material existence. This is not the evidence of recent research, although Max Tegmark has attempted to demonstrate that timescales operating internally within the brain are in excess of ten orders of magnitude longer than timescales associated with leakage from quantum systems – a process known as 'decoherence'. This again only works as an argument if quantum processes are excluded altogether as existing in the workings of the brain. But quantum processes, even including antimatter occurrences, are not excluded from any part of existence and their characteristics of connectivity indicate that there is no such thing as nothing, across which connections are somehow made. Micro space, through (and by) which quantum mechanics operate, is not entirely empty. Mediums of sorts are posited to exist through which electromagnetic waves must pass. That being so, connectivity at quantum scales involves shared use of space with the existence of other exotic particles both within and at its numerous boundaries. The argument boils down to quantum isolationism from anything else versus connectivity with everything.

And so God lives to fight another day.

If natural selection is now becoming insufficient, too, as a concept to explain the totality of life forms, and needs modification, or even replacement, then Crick's own dismissal of anything which challenged that boundary might serve also to undermine his more strident dismissal of religion.

Monarchy has the advantage over the centuries of seeing plenty of such apparently conclusive explanations challenged as science advances, and royal prayer has continued through it all. The new field of neurotheology will have plenty to offer to our understanding of the brain's workings, but it would be a foolish scientist who dismisses the existence of as yet unknown forces in the workings of life. Profesor Dawkins's work published in 2006 called *The God Delusion* thus falls straight into this trap.

God has survived numerous such apparently fatal attacks from scientists armed with new knowledge over the years, as one theory has been modified by another, or overtaken entirely, and so the occasional church service is still held by the Sovereign for Members of the Order of Merit. During this service the following reading, authorized personally by The Queen for use upon this occasion, is customarily read by the Duke of Edinburgh:

Wisdom is an inexhaustible treasure for mankind, and those who profit by it become God's friends, commended to him by the gifts they derive from her instruction.

God grant that I may speak according to his will, and that my own thoughts may be worthy of his gifts; for even wisdom is under God's direction and he corrects the wise; we and our words, prudence and knowledge and craftsmanship, all are in his hand. He himself gave me true understanding of things as they are: a knowledge of the structure of the world and the operation of the elements; the beginning and the end of epochs and their middle course; the alternating solstices and changing seasons; the cycles of the years and the constellations; the nature of living creatures and behaviour of wild beasts; the violent force of winds and the thoughts of men; the varieties of plants and the virtues of roots. I learnt it all, hidden or manifest, for I was taught by her whose skill made all things, wisdom.[10]

Notes

[1] Wis. 6.21.

[2] W. Ford Doolittle claimed, controversially in 1999, that: 'molecular phylogenists will have failed to find the "true tree", not because their methods are inadequate or because they have chosen the wrong genes, but because the history of life cannot properly be represented as a tree' and that 'The tree of life is not something that exists in nature, it's way that humans classify nature': W. Ford Doolittle (1999), 'Phylogenetic Classification and the Universal Tree', *Science*, 284 (25 June): 2124–8.

[3] *New Scientist* (2009), 'Uprooting Darwin's Tree', 24 January, p. 39.

[4] *New Scientist* (2009), 'Uprooting Darwin's Tree', 24 January, p. 39.

[5] Simon Conway Morris interviewed in *New Scientist* (2009), 'Evolution's Final Frontiers', 31 January, p. 43.

[6] Einstein's Foreword to C. P. Hapgood's, *Earth's Shifting Crust: A Key to Some Basic Problems of Earth Science* (New York: Pantheon Books, 1958), pp. 1–2. The Foreword was written in 1953.

[7] Einstein's Foreword to C. P. Hapgood's, *Earth's Shifting Crust: A Key to some Basic Problems of Earth Science* (New York: Pantheon Books, 1958), pp. 1–2. The Foreword was written in 1953.

[8] T. Maudlin, *Quantum Non-Locality and Relativity: Metaphysical Intimations of Modern Physics* (2nd edn), (Oxford: Wiley-Blackwell, 2002).

[9] V. Stenger, *Quantum Gods: Creation, Chaos and the Search for Cosmic Consciousness* (Amherst, NY: Prometheus Books, 2009).

[10] Wis. 7, within 'Service of Thanksgiving for Members of the Order of Merit', Archive of Her Majesty's Chapel Royal, St James's Palace.

Appendix

Royal Military Prayers

Royal Collects in present prayers of the Armed Forces of the Crown:

The Royal Navy

O Eternal Lord God, who alone spreadest out the heavens, and rulest the raging of the sea; who has compassed the waters with bounds until day and night come to an end: be pleased to receive into thy Almighty and most gracious protection the persons of us thy servants, and the Fleet which we serve. Preserve us from the dangers of the sea and of the air, and from the violence of the enemy; that we may be a safeguard unto our most gracious Sovereign Lady, Queen Elizabeth and her Dominions, and a security for such as pass on the seas upon their lawful occasions; that the inhabitants of our Island and Commonwealth may in peace and quietness serve thee our God; and that we may return in safety to enjoy the blessings of the land, with the fruits of our labours; and with a thankful remembrance of thy mercies to praise and glorify thy Holy Name; through Jesus Christ our Lord. Amen.

The Royal Marines

O Eternal Lord God, who through many generations has united and inspired the members of our Corps, grant thy blessing, we beseech thee, on Royal Marines serving all round the globe. Bestow thy crown of righteousness upon all our efforts and endeavours, and may our laurels be those of gallantry and honour, loyalty and courage. We ask these things in the name of him whose courage never failed, our Redeemer Jesus Christ. Amen.

The Army

Collects of the Regiments and Corps of the British Army authorized by the Chaplain-General of Her Majesty's Land Forces

A consequence of the government's 'Options for Change' introduced in the 1990s to reorganize the structure of the Army was to render redundant many favourite prayers formulated in 1930 by the Revd. Matthew Tobias, published as *Collects of the British Army'*, and used alike for formal structured worship and at Drumhead services on the battlefield through the Second World War and thereafter, until updated in 1976 by the Chaplain General in the form of *The Black Book*. This amended the Tobias collation so as to incorporate mid-century amalgamations of Army units, and newly written collects. 'Options for Change' necessitated a whole new swathe of Collects to cope with large-scale disbandment or amalgamation of regiments and units of the Army in an attempt to 'cash in' on what was perceived to be the peace dividend at the fall of the Iron Curtain. However, conflicts continued to break out and some to intensify to levels not seen since the Second World War, and a further reorganization was devised in response as the 'Future Army Structure' (FAS) in 2007. The Revd R.A. McDowall worked to keep up with these changes and the following are now officially authorized and issued by the Chaplain General for current use by the British Army. In order of regimental precedence they represent the Sovereign's wish as Colonel-in-Chief of the Armed Forces of The Crown.

The Life Guards

O Ever-living God, King of Kings, in whose service we put on the breastplate of faith and love, and for a helmet the hope of salvation, grant we beseech thee that The Life Guards may be faithful unto death, and at last receive the crown of life from Jesus Christ, our Lord. Amen.

Formed in April 1922 from The 1st Life Guards and The 2nd Life Guards, and took their present title in June 1928.

The Blues and Royals

O Lord Jesus Christ who by the Holy Apostle has called us to put on the armour of God and to take the sword of the spirit, give thy grace we pray thee, to the Blues and Royals that we may fight manfully under thy banner against all evil, and waiting on thee to renew our strength, may mount up with wings as eagles, in thy name, who livest and reignest with the Father and the Holy Ghost, ever one God, world without end. Amen.

Formed on 29 March 1969 from The Royal Horse Guards (The Blues) and The Royal Dragoons (1st Dragoons).

The Royal Armoured Corps

Almighty God, who art our defence and our castle, grant to the Royal Armoured Corps that putting on the whole armour of God they may go forth through the earth eager to do thee service with courage and faith, and never be separated from thy grace or divided among themselves, through Jesus Christ Our Lord to whom, with the Father and Holy Spirit one blessed and eternal Trinity, be glory for ever. Amen.

Formed on the 29 March 1967 from all line Cavalry Regiments and the Royal Tank Regiment.

1st The Queen's Dragoon Guards

O Lord God, whose throne is in heaven and whose eyes behold the children of men, grant that as thy prophet saw the valiant horse eager to go forth through the earth on thy service, so may the Queen's Dragoon Guards, united in keeping thy Royal Law and thinking no evil in their hearts, ever seek to serve their Sovereign and their native land in thee and for thee, who art one God, world without end. Amen.

Formed on 1 January 1959-from 1st King's Dragoon Guards and The Queen's Bays (2nd Dragoon Guards)

The Royal Scots Dragoon Guards

Almighty God, whose blessed Son, Jesus Christ, gave us a perfect pattern of service, give us grace that we, the Royal Scots Dragoon Guards, may be second to none in following his example, swifter than eagles to overtake his enemies and serve thee in thine everlasting Kingdom, through the same Jesus Christ Our Lord. Amen.

Formed on 2 July 1971 from 3rd Caribiniers (Prince of Wales's Dragoon Guards) and The Royal Scots Greys (2nd Dragoons).

The Queen's Royal Hussars

Almighty God, whose perfect love casteth out fear, remember in thy great goodness the Queen's Royal Hussars and all who serve with us. Keep us mindful of former valour, and grant us thy grace, that whatsoever our minds and hands shall find to do for thee, we may endure hardships as thy good and faithful soldiers, and so enter into thy glory, through Jesus Christ our Lord. Amen.

Formed on 1 August 1992 from 4th/7th Royal Dragoon Guards and 5th Royal Inniskilling Dragoon Guards.

9th/12th Royal Lancers

O Eternal God, grant to us, thy servants of the 9th/12th Royal Lancers, strength, guidance, courage and steadfast Faith, that we may ever serve thee truly; and finally by thy mercy attain everlasting glory, through Jesus Christ our Lord. Amen.

Formed on 11 September 1960 from 9th Queen's Royal Lancers and 12th Royal Lancers (Prince of Wales's).

The King's Royal Hussars

Almighty God, by whose power and in whose mercy we are shielded from danger and pardoned when we have done wrong, help us all, as members of the King's Royal Hussars, to find in our service in the Regiment a sure way of serving thee. Help us to dedicate our lives in that we may live for others rather than ourselves, and grant that through the power of the Holy Spirit we may be steadfast in duty, patient in hardship and bold at all times to declare the truth in the name of him who loves us and died for us, Jesus Christ our Lord. Amen.

The Light Dragoons

Almighty God, who givest more than we desire or deserve, grant to us the Light Dragoons, that we who strive for our Queen and country may serve thee with one heart and mind, in true fellowship with each other. And grant that we may never count the cost but in all things loyally fulfil thy Royal Law and at the last attain the glory of thy salvation; this we ask through the merit of him who is the Resurrection and the Life, even our Lord Jesus Christ.

Formed on 1 December 1992 from 13th/18th Royal Hussars (Queen Mary's Own) and 15th/19th The King's Royal Hussars.

The Queen's Royal Lancers

Almighty God, our Heavenly Father, grant (we pray) to thy faithful soldiers of the Queen's Royal Lancers thy strength and courage; that united in our duty to pursue thy peace, we may at the last pass through death to thy eternal glory, for the sake of Jesus Christ our Lord. Amen.

Formed on 25 June 1993 from 16th/5th Queen's Royal Lancers and 17th/21st Lancers.

The Royal Tank Regiment

Almighty God, whose perfect love casteth out fear, mercifully grant that thy servants of the Royal Tank Regiment may fear naught but to fall from thy favour, for his sake, in whom thou art well pleased, thy beloved Son, Jesus Christ our Lord. Amen.

For The Royal Tank Corps renamed on 4 April 1939.

The Royal Regiment of Artillery

O Lord Jesus Christ, who dost everywhere lead thy people in the way of righteousness, vouchsafe so to lead the Royal Regiment of Artillery that wherever we serve, on land or sea or in the air, we may win the glory of doing thy will. Amen.

The Royal Engineers

O God, whose righteousness is exceeding glorious, may it please thee to send out thy light and thy truth to lead us thy servants of the Corps of Royal Engineers that everywhere we may be enabled to do our duty, and so may glorify thee our Father in Heaven, for the sake of Jesus Christ our Lord. Amen.

The Royal Corps of Signals

Almighty God, whose messengers go forth in every age giving light and understanding grant that we of the Royal Corps of Signals, who speed the word of man to man, may be swift and sure in sending the message of thy truth into all the world. May we serve thee faithfully and, with the help of thy Holy Spirit, make such success of our soldierly duties on this earth that we may be found worthy to receive the crown of life hereafter, through Jesus Christ our Lord. Amen.

The Grenadier Guards

O God grant that thy servants, the Grenadier Guards, may ever be mindful of their proud and costly heritage, that continuing to guard what is right, and fighting for what is just, they may so serve thee here in this life that they may be counted worthy to join those who now continue their service in the life to come; through Jesus Christ our Lord. Amen.

The Coldstream Guards

Eternal Lord, beside whom there is no God, keep, we pray thee, the Coldstream Guards second to none in loyal duty to thine only begotten Son, our Lord Jesus Christ, who with Thee, O Father and with the Holy Ghost, liveth and reigneth one God,world without end. Amen.

The Scots Guards

Almighty God, whose blessed Son did say unto Saint Andrew 'Follow me', grant that the Scots Guards, who wear the Cross of thy Holy Apostle, may follow thy Son with impunity; be made stronger in brotherhood and fierce against all enemies of our Saviour, ever going forward under the leadership of him, who by the hard and painful way of the cross, won high conquest and great glory, even Jesus Christ our Lord. Amen.

The Irish Guards

Almighty God, who through the glory of the eternal Trinity hast inspired men in every age to love and serve thee, and hast promised that none shall be separated from thy love who truly trust in thee; we beseech thee thou wouldst keep thy servants the Irish Guards steadfast in this faith, that they may show it forth not only with their lips but in their lives, who livest and reignest, one God, world without end. Amen.

The Welsh Guards

O Lord God, who hast given us the land of our fathers for our inheritance, help thy servants, the Welsh Guards, to keep thy laws as our heritage for ever, until we come to that better and heavenly country which thou hast prepared for us; through Jesus Christ our Lord. Amen.

O Arglwdd Dduw, a roddaist i ni wlad ein tadau yn draftadaeth, cynorthwya dy weision, y Gwarchodlu Cymreig, i gadw Dy ddeddfau yn etifeddiaeth inni dros fyth, nes y down i'r wlad well a nefol a baratoaist i ni, trwy Iesu Grist ein Harglwydd.

The Royal Regiment of Scotland

God of our fathers, whose hand shapes the coastlands and hills of home, fashion likewise our lives. Guard the Royal Regiment of Scotland;keep us brave in battle, resolute in adversity, loyal to comrade and Crown; that inspired by the faith and cross of St. Andrew, we might secure lasting peace and eternal rest; through Jesus Christ our Saviour. Amen.

The Princess of Wales's Royal Regiment (Queen's and Royal Hampshires)

Almighty God, the strength of those who put their trust in thee and the hope of those who serve and follow thee; grant to the members of the Princess of Wales's Royal Regiment such a measure of thy grace that in both peace and war they may win thy favour, and with courage and loyalty faithfully serve their Queen and country, upholding those noble traditions of which they are the proud inheritors. We ask this for the sake of Jesus Christ our Lord. Amen.

The Royal Regiment of Fusiliers

O God our guide from of old, grant that wherever thy servants of the Royal Regiment of Fusiliers are called upon to serve, we may follow the example of thy servant St George and ever prove steadfast in Faith and valiant in Battle, through him who is the Captain of our Salvation, Jesus Christ our Lord. Amen.

The Royal Anglian Regiment

O Lord God, who by the brightness of a star didst lead men to the Saviour of mankind; give thy grace to the Royal Anglian Regiment, that trusting in thee as our strong rock and castle, we may in unity with thee and with one another rightly serve our Sovereign and our native land, and at the last be led by thy mercy to thy heavenly kingdom, through Jesus Christ our Lord. Amen.

The Duke of Lancaster's Regiment (King's, Lancashire and Border)

O Lord Jesus, who began to build the Kingdom of God upon earth through a company of men, grant that we who are Kingsmen may never cease to be your servants. Let no difficulties daunt us, for we shall be your soldiers and you shall be our God so that, being loyal until death, we may come at last to your everlasting kingdom, where you are one with the Father and the Holy Spirit, world without end. Amen.

The Yorkshire Regiment (14th/15th, 19th and 33rd/76th Foot)

O Lord God, the shield and buckler of all that trust Thee: grant to the Yorkshire Regiment, in its Battalions and ranks, the strength that fears no evil tidings, no desperate endeavours and no foe bodily or spiritual; but advances in Thy righteousness through all rough places, under the Captain of our Salvation, Jesus Christ our Lord. Amen.

The Mercian Regiment

Almighty God, Lord and giver of life, who delivers us from the bonds of sin and enables us to fight the good fight of Faith; knot together your servants of the Mercian Regiment, that calling to mind the valour of their forbears, and being rooted in the love of their brothers, they may stand firm as a forest of oak and strike hard against all dangers and adversities; for the sake of Jesus Christ our Lord. Amen.

The Royal Welsh

Eternal God, our heavenly Father, who gave your Son Jesus Christ to die for us and raised him up from the dead; uphold, we pray, the ancient valour of the Royal Welsh, that we may ever follow the path of duty after His example and by his grace be found worthy of your eternal Kingdom through the same Jesus Christ our Lord. Amen.

Dragwyddol Dduw, ein Tad nefol, a roddaist dy Fab Iesu Grist i farw drosom a'i godi o'r meirw; erfyniwn arnat gynnal gwroldeb hynafol y Cymry Brenhinol, fel y gallwn bob amser ddilyn llwybr dyletswydd yn ôl ei Esiampl a thrwy Ei ras fod yn deilwng o'th Deyrnas dragwyddol; drwy'r un Iesu Grist ein Harglwydd. Amen.

The Rifles

O Almighty God, the sure stronghold of each succeeding age, guard us your servants of The Rifles, that we may uphold and be worthy of the great traditions of our former Regiments; and as we were chosen to be swift and bold, may we seek with courage your grace in every time of need, and so be patient and persevere in running the race that is set before us, as did your Son Jesus Christ, our Lord. Amen.

The Royal Irish Regiment & The Royal Irish Rangers

Almighty God, whose love knows no bounds, grant that we, the Royal Irish Regiment, may do our duty courageously whether at home or abroad, so that undaunted by the difficulties which beset us, your will may be done And united as members one with another, may we, mindful of the valour and sacrifice of those who have gone before us, clear the way for those that follow; through Jesus Christ, our Lord. Amen.

The Parachute Regiment

May the defence of the Most High be above and beneath around and within us, in our going out and in our coming in, in our rising up and in our going down, through all our days and all our nights, until the dawn when the Sun of righteousness shall arise with healing in his wings for the peoples of the world; through Jesus Christ our Lord. Amen.

The Christian Personnel of the Brigade of Gurkhas

Almighty God, Father of all, whose ancient people looked to the hills, grant to us of the Brigade of Gurkhas, bound together in a bond of friendship, that we may serve our Sovereign with loyalty, integrity and cheerfulness; and mindful of our traditions, may we swiftly follow wherever you lead, and so at the last come to our eternal home, for the sake of him who called his disciples his friends, even Jesus Christ our Lord. Amen.

The Royal Gurkha Rifles formed 1 July 1994 from 2nd King Edward VII's Own Gurkha Rifles (The Sirmoor Rifles), 6th Queen Elizabeth's Own Gurkha Rifles, 7th Duke of Edinburgh's Own Gurkha Rifles, 10th Princess Mary's Own Gurkha Rifles, The Queen 's Gurkha Engineers, The Queen's Gurkha Signals and The Queen's Own Gurkha Transport Regiment.

The London Regiment

Most merciful Father, by whom we live and move and have our being, grant to us of The London Regiment your help to defend the right; so that, mindful of our heritage, undivided in loyalty to our sovereign and directed aright, we may at last clear the way to enter the Heavenly City; through the merits of your son, Jesus Christ our Lord. Amen.

The Special Air Service Regiment

O Lord who didst call on thy disciples to venture all to win all men to thee, grant that we, the chosen members of the Special Air Service Regiment, may by our works and ways dare all to win all, and in doing so render special service to thee and our fellow-men in all the world, through the same Jesus Christ our Lord. Amen.

The Army Air Corps

Almighty God, who makest the clouds thy chariots, and who walkest upon the wings of the wind, have mercy upon all who serve in the Army Air Corps that they may have the assurance of your presence with them, and find thy hand to support and strengthen them, through Jesus Christ our Lord. Amen.

The Royal Army Chaplains' Department

Blessed God, who has committed the glorious Gospel to our trust, have mercy upon the Royal Army Chaplains' Department and grant that we may never glory save in the Cross of our Lord Jesus Christ, but in all things may approve ourselves as your ministers, through. the same your Son Jesus Christ our Lord. Amen.

Bendigaid Dduw, a ymddiriedaist yr Efengyl ogoneddus i'n gofal, bydd yn drugarog wrth Adran Frenhinol Caplaniaid y Fyddin, a phar na ogoneddwn mewn dim oddieithr Croes ein Harglwydd Iesu Grist, ac y cawn ym mhob peth ein cymer-adwyo fel dy weinidogion, trwy yr un Iesu Grist dy Fab Ein Harglwydd. Amen.

The Royal Logistic Corps

God our Father, whose Son Jesus Christ ministered to the needs of mankind, may we of the Royal Logistic Corps, so tackle the diverse tasks assigned to us; that wherever we serve, on land or sea, or in the air we may sustain our comrades both in peace and war, and thus be found worthy of those whom we seek to support, for the sake of Jesus Christ our Lord. Amen.

Formed on 5 April 1993 from: Royal Engineers (Postal and Courier), Royal Corps of Transport, Royal Army Ordnance Corps, Royal Pioneer Corps and Army Catering Corps.

The Royal Army Medical Corps

O God, whose blessed Son was made perfect though suffering, give thy grace, we beseech thee, to thy servants of the Royal Army Medical Corps, that by loyalty in hard service after the example of Saint Luke the beloved physician, we may be found faithful in ministering to those that need, for his sake who went about doing good, the same thy Son Jesus Christ our Lord. Amen.

The Corps of Royal Electrical and Mechanical Engineers

O God of power and might, whose all-pervading energy is the strength of nature and man, inspire, we pray Thee, us Thy servants of the Royal Electrical and Mechanical Engineers with the quickening spirit of goodwill, that as honest craftsmen, seeking only the good of all in peace or war, we may glorify Thee both in the work of our hands and the example of our fellowship, through Jesus Christ our Lord. Amen.

Adjutant General's Corps (All Branches)

Father of all, grant to us who are bound together in the Adjutant General's Corps, the grace to understand that those whom we support depend on our integrity, expertise and resolution; and, following in the footsteps of your Son, may we be mindful of their needs and faithful in our responsibilities; through the same Jesus Christ our Lord. Amen.

Adjutant General's Corps (Staff and Personnel Support Branch)

Almighty God, Creator and Father of all, so direct our lives that we may serve with integrity and resolution in the Adjutant General's Corps; and grant that in our service we may ever be worthy of the trust of those whom we seek to support for the sake of Jesus Christ our Lord. Amen.

Formed on 6 April 1992 from Staff and Regimental Clerks, Royal Army Pay Corps and Women's Royal Army Corps.

Adjutant General's Corps Provost Branch (Royal Military Police)

Almighty God, by whose grace we are called to positions of responsibility and trust bless, we pray thee, all members of the Royal Military Police (and those who previously served in the Corps of Royal Military Police). Inspire them to courage and wisdom, courtesy and faithfulness: grant them a true knowledge of thy will that they may guide their comrades aright: that by saving others in justice and mercy they may also serve thee and so become more worthy of their calling; through Jesus Christ our Lord. Amen.

Formed on 6 April 1992 from personnel of The Corps of Royal Military Police.

Adjutant General's Corps Provost Branch (Military Provost Branch)

Almighty God, whose ways are justice and peace and whose judgements are righteous and merciful, grant to us they servants of the Military Provost Staff (and those who previously served in the Military Provost Staff Corps*) the spirit of understanding and compassion, that by thy inspiration we may be faithful in the discharge of our duties, zealous in protection of the weak and faint-hearted and selfless in serving the best interest of those who have been committed to our charge. We ask this in the Name, and in the service, of our Lord and Saviour, Jesus Christ. Amen.

Formed on 6 April 1992 from personnel of The Military Provost Staff Corps.

* To be included on appropriate occasions.

Adjutant General's Corps (Education and Training Services)

Almighty God, whose word giveth light in the darkness, grant to us thy servants of the Educational and Training Services Branch (and those who previously served in the Royal Army Educational Corps*) that with steadfast hands we may carry amongst soldiers the torch of learning and that with thine aid, both we and they may gain not only knowledge but wisdom, and may come to understand more clearly thy purpose for mankind. May we discern thy presence everywhere in nature and in the minds of men, so that our teaching may bear constant witness to him, who is the Way, the Truth and the Life; through Jesus Christ our Lord. Amen.

Formed on 6 April 1992 from personnel of The Royal Army Education Corps.

Adjutant General's Corps (Army Legal Services)

Almighty God, before whom we shall all be judged at the last day, grant to us of the Army Legal Services (and to those who previously served in the Army Legal Corps*) that we may prosecute justice with integrity and truth, and also defend the rights of those committed to our care; so that at the last we may obtain mercy under your judgement; through Jesus Christ our Lord. Amen.

Formed on 6 April 1992 from personnel of The Army Legal Corps.

* To be included on appropriate occasions.

Royal Veterinary Corps

O God, who didst create man in thine own image, and gavest him dominion over every living thing, give wisdom and grace, we pray thee, to thy servants of the Royal Army Veterinary Corps, that we may guard these thy creatures committed to our care against disease and suffering and promote their health and usefulness; and may ever declare both by word and example that the merciful man is kind to his beast, for his sake, who has told us that not one sparrow is forgotten before thee, Jesus Christ our merciful Redeemer. Amen.

Small Arms School Corps

Almighty God, who alone canst strengthen us in the hour of danger, and inspire us to fight the good fight of Faith; give, we pray thee, to thy servants of the Small Arms School Corps, whose service it is to teach our comrades against the day of battle, faithfulness and zeal in this their duty May they ever be mindful of that other warfare of the Spirit and prove themselves We warriors of thy Eternal Kingdom; through Jesus Christ our Lord. Amen.

The Royal Dental Corps

O God, who art the source of man's best gifts, grant to us who serve in the Royal Army Dental Corps wisdom and under-standing, that our minds may seek further knowledge and our hands lose not their ability and skills; so that we may serve thee in promoting health of body and peace of mind for those in our care; we ask this in the name of him who is the health and peace of all thy servants, Jesus Christ our Lord. Amen.

Intelligence Corps

O God, who alone givest true wisdom: grant to thy servants of the Intelligence Corps such gifts of understanding and truth, that by their vigilance thy people may live their lives in freedom and in peace to thy glory and the welfare of this realm; for thy Holy name's sake. Amen.

Army Physical Training Corps

O God, whose will it is that mind, body and spirit should work in unity to thy glory, help us of the Army Physical Training Corps to serve thee in our work and ever to remember that the body must be the servant of the mind, and the mind the servant of the spirit, and that only as they obtain their strength from thee can their purpose be fulfilled and thy name be glorified: through Jesus Christ our Lord. Amen.

Queen Alexandra's Royal Nursing Corps

O God, who through the healing touch of thy dear Son didst recover the sick and relieve their pain, grant to us who serve beneath thy Cross in the Queen Alexandra's Royal Army Nursing Corps such love towards thee and devotion to our duty that the shadows may pass from those entrusted to our care, their darkness lighten into faith and hope, and thy love bring healing peace, for his sake who was content to suffer for all mankind, even Jesus Christ our Lord. Amen.

Formed on1 February 1949 from personnel of Queen Alexandra's Imperial Military Nursing Service.

Army Medical Services

Almighty and everlasting God, who sent your son, Jesus Christ, to be Saviour and Healer of men; we ask you to bless the work of the Army Medical Services. Grant that we who are called to share in this ministry of healing may ever have present in our minds the example of our Lord, and his tenderness and sympathy for all human suffering Give us grace and patience faithfully to fulfil our calling and crown our work with good success; for the love of your Son, Jesus Christ, our Lord. Amen.

This Collect may be used when personnel from two or more Corps of the AMS (RAMC, RADC, QARANC and RAVC) are present, in place of individual Corps Collects.

The School of Infantry

Almighty God, who alone can strengthen us in the hour of danger, give to thy servants of the School of Infantry, whose service it is to teach their comrades against the day of battle, faithfulness and zeal in this their duty. May they ever be mindful of the greater warfare of the Spirit, so that, filled with thy power, they may prove true leaders in the battle for thy eternal kingdom, through Jesus Christ our Lord. Amen.

The Staff College

Almighty God, bless, we pray thee, all those who work at the Staff College .Grant that they and their families may make the most of their opportunities; give them patience and under-standing, energy and good humour; and help them always to remember that the wisdom of the Owl and the power of the Sword are nothing without thy grace and the strength of thy Holy Spirit. Amen.

The Royal Military College of Science

O God, the source of all knowledge and wisdom, bless we beseech thee the work of the Royal Military College of Science and grant to all who labour therein the enlightenment of thy Holy Spirit, that in their search for truth they may discover the hidden purposes of thy creation and so be led into the way of faith and service, to thy glory and the benefit of all mankind; through Jesus Christ our Lord. Amen.

The Royal Military Academy Sandhurst

Almighty God, whose Son, the Lord of all life, came not to be served but to serve; help us to be masters of ourselves that we may be the servants of others, and teach us to serve to lead; through the same Jesus Christ our Lord. Amen.

The Royal Hospital Chelsea

O God, who by the overshadowing of an oak didst preserve our Royal Founder from the hands of his enemies and so lead him to an earthly throne, grant thy heavenly protection, we beseech thee, to thy servants in this Royal Hospital, that continuing in thy love, they may give thee true and loyal service, and so enduring to the end enter at the last into thine eternal kingdom in glory, through the merits of Jesus Christ, our Lord and Saviour. Amen.

The Army Cadet Force

Our God our Father, who hast brought us together as members of the Army Cadet Force; help us to do our duty at all times and to be loyal to each other. May all that is good and true prosper among us; strengthen us to defend the right, and bless our work that it may be acceptable to thee; for Jesus Christ's sake. Amen.

The Royal Air Force

The Royal Air Force Collect 1

Almighty God, who has promised that they who wait upon thee shall renew their strength and mount up with wings, as eagles, we commend to thy fatherly protection all who serve in the Royal Air Force. Uplift and support us in our endeavour, that we may be a safeguard unto our most gracious Sovereign Lady Queen Elizabeth and a sure defence to our homeland. Help us to fulfil our several duties with honour, goodwill and integrity, and grant that we may prove to be worthy successors of those who by their valour and sacrifice did nobly save their day and generation; through Jesus Christ our Lord. Amen.

The Royal Air Force Collect 2

Almighty God, who makest the clouds thy chariots and walkest upon the wings of the storm, look in mercy we beseech thee upon the Royal Air Force. Make us a tower of strength to our Queen and to our country. Help us to do our duty with prudence and with fearlessness, confident that in life or in death the eternal God is our refuge and strength. Grant this for Jesus Christ's sake. Amen.

The Royal Air Force Collect 3

O Holy Spirit, Breath of God, who dost inspire and sustain man's destiny, quicken we beseech Thee, the hearts and minds of all who serve in the Royal Air Force; that those who fly may brave the perils of the air with courage; that those who labour on the ground may be infused with zeal and devotion; and that all who bear the burden and heat of the day may be refreshed with the live-giving power of thy grace; through Jesus Christ our Lord. Amen.

The Royal Air Force Regiment

Almighty God, Lord of heaven and earth, whose son Jesus Christ showed us the path of duty, we beseech thee to bless all who serve in the Royal Air Force Regiment. Help us to do our duty with courage and dedication. Of thy goodness be our strength in times of danger, watch over our loved ones when we are separated, and make us a sure defence to those we serve. We ask this in the name of Jesus Christ our Lord. Amen.

The Guild of St Helena

O Lord Jesus Christ, who by thy cross didst triumph over death, and by thy resurrection didst open unto us the Kingdom of Heaven; bless we beseech thee, the Guild of St Helena and us the members in our work, and grant that we may ever rejoice in the hope of eternal life; through thy grace, who with the Father and the Holy Spirit, livest and reignest, ever one God, world without end.

The Queen's Body Guard of the Yeomen of The Guard (founded 1485, Bosworth Field)

This Collect for the Yeomen of The Guard, drafted by The Revd Prebendary William Scott, Sub-Dean of HM Chapels Royal, was officially approved for use at the 500th Anniversary of the death of their founder, King Henry VII, at Westminster Abbey on 28 April 2009, and is now adopted as the official Collect to be used in perpetuity:

Almighty God, who art the protector of all that thou hast made, and who hast entrusted thy servants the Yeomen of the Guard with the protection of our Gracious Sovereign: grant that they may perform their duties with dignity and prowess, seeking to fear God and to honour The Queen; through Jesus Christ our Lord. Amen.

Her Majesty's Body Guard of The Honourable Corps of Gentlemen-at-Arms (founded 1509 by King Henry VIII)

This Collect was drafted in 2009 by Colonel The Revd Richard Whittington and approved by The Queen for the 500th Anniversary of the raising of the King's Spears and Gentlemen-at-Arms by King Henry VIII in 1509, and for use in perpetuity:

Almighty God, our heavenly Father, King of kings and Lord of lords, who hast taught us that in serving one another we are serving Thee: Direct and strengthen us, the Honourable Corps of Gentlemen-at-Arms, that through loyal and dedicated service as 'Nearest Guard' to our earthly Sovereign, we may render unfailing service to Thee, our Sovereign Lord. Grant this, O merciful Father through Jesus Christ our Lord.

Index

Iliana, Princess Iliana of
Romania 105, 109, 120n 1
see also Mother Alexandra
India 2, 44, 84, 122, 132, 155,
164–5
Indian Famine Relief Fund
(1897) 125

James, The Reverend Graham 92
James de Rohano Stuardo (alleged
son of King Charles II) 50,
52, 60n 2, 65
James (King James VI of
Scotland) 82, 96, 99, 101n 1
Jefferson, Thomas 72, 80, 81n 5
Joao II (King of Portugal) 1–2
Jodrell Bank 159–60
Juliana (Queen of the
Netherlands) 24

Kelly, Edward 44
Kensington Palace 17, 140, 163
Key, Francis Scott 79–80, 81n 2,
90
Khrushchev, Nikita 166
Kingsbridge 27
Kipling, Rudyard 143–4
Knox, John 42–4, 48n 1

La Peyrere, Isaac 157
Lambeth Conference Resolution
(1948)127
Lang, John 33–4
Lancaster, Joseph 125–6
Lascelles, Tommy 92, 103n 11
Laud, Bishop William (*see* London,
Bishops)
Laurence, Vice Admiral
Timothy 147
L'Enfant, Pierre Charles 72
Lenin, Vladimir Ilyich Ulyanov
(1870–1924) 107, 112
Nadezhola Konstantinova
Krupskaya107
Les Invalides 54–5
Liber Regalis x, xivn 5
Lincoln, Abraham 74–5
London, Bishops of
Richard Chartres, Bishop of,

and Dean of Chapel
Royal 18–19
William Laud, Bishop of, and
Dean of Chapel Royal 44–5,
47
London Nautical School 23
Louis Philippe (Orleans, King of
France 1830–48) 54, 55
Louis, Prince Imperial 58–9
Lovell, Sir Bernard 159–60
Lynmouth 99
Lytlington, Nicholas (Abbot) x,
xivn 5

Ma Tsu 153–4
Maclean, Donald 20–1, 26n 9, 162
McCrea, John 141
McFarlane, Frank, 168, 170n 9
McGonnegal, William 27
McKinley, William (1843–1901)
75, 79
Madison, James (1751–1836) 80
Magellan, Ferdinand 2, 156
Malta 4, 7, 143
Manorwater papers 63
Marbeuf, Compte de (Gov. of
Corsica) 49
Margaret Rose, HRH Princess
86–7, 101
Marlborough, HMS 92
Mars, HMS 28–30
Marti (*see* Standart)
Marx, Karl 31–3, 37n 5–6, 112, 128
Mary, of Modena (Queen Consort)
39
Masons
Monumental Mason to The
Crown 141
Rosicrucian 72
Templar 72
Massilan, Marguerite (Comtesse
de) 65
Meath, Earl of 122
Merchant Naval Service of
Remembrance23
Methuen, Treaty (1703) 40
Millennium Bridge
London ('Wobbly') 35–6
Newcastle 35